THANK YOU!

FOR GETTING YOUR COPY OF
SELL 100+ HOMES A YEAR

You've made a **great decision**, and I'm so excited to give you this copy of Sell 100+ Homes A Year! This book will help you change your business, and learn to do business differently than you ever thought possible.

As you learn to embrace teachnology and implement the techniques in this book, I want you to know that you are not alone! We have a group of like minded Real Estate professionals like yourself who are looking to make major changes in the industry. We'd love for you to come join us, so we can help you gain massive momentum in your business.

You can join our community,
7 Figure Realtor Blueprint here:
www.facebook.com/groups/7figurerealtorblueprint/

When you come, please take a picture of yourself holding up this book, and post that picture in our group introducing yourself to our group and use the hashtag #sell100homes in the post.

Thanks again for getting your copy, and I can't wait to start telling your success story.

For the resources mentioned in this book, please visit

https://sell100homesbook.com/join

SELL

100+

HOMES

A YEAR

How We Use Engagement Marketing,
Technology and Lead Gen to
Sell 100+ Homes A Year, *Every* Year!

BY KRISTA MASHORE

Published by Best Seller Publishing®, Pasadena, CA
Best Seller Publishing® is a registered trademark
Printed in the United States of America.

This publication is designed to provide accurate and authoritative information with regard to the subject matter covered. It is sold with the understanding that the publisher is not engaged in rendering legal, accounting, or other professional advice. If legal advice or other expert assistance is required, the services of a competent professional should be sought. The opinions expressed by the authors in this book are not endorsed by Best Seller Publishing® and are the sole responsibility of the author rendering the opinion.

Most Best Seller Publishing® titles are available at special quantity discounts for bulk purchases for sales promotions, premiums, fundraising, and educational use. Special versions or book excerpts can also be created to fit specific needs.

For more information, please write:
Best Seller Publishing®
1346 Walnut Street, #205
Pasadena, CA 91106
or call 1(626) 765 9750
Toll Free: 1(844) 850-3500
Visit us online at: www.BestSellerPublishing.org

Acknowledgements

First and foremost, I would like to thank my husband Steve Mashore and my three children Jaynlin, Kayli and Casey for standing by me for so many years. I know I've worked super long hours and it seems like my phone is attached to me. Please know when I'm away at my trainings and workshops, you are always on my mind. I know there were to many times that I worked during vacations and I haven't always been as mentally present as I needed to be, but please know I will continually work on that. Thank all of you for loving me, understanding my crazy drive and ambition, and for supporting my constant love of learning. I promise I'll continue working on being the best mom and wife I can be. I am truly blessed to have such a loving and devoted family.

Thank you to the people who made me the woman and businesswoman I am today: My dad who gave me the confidence, love and support. I don't think any other human being sees in me what you do. And my mom, whose loyalty, ethics and integrity has impacted everything I do.

Also, thanks to Cathy Cross and Josh Vitale - I love you like crazy! You helped me expand Homes by Krista which has allowed me the time to create my coaching program. Your commitment and passion to serving people is a role model for all professionals in our industry.

Thanks to my amazing team for putting all my learning into action. I appreciate that you as a team always strive for better - and that you don't freak out when I return from a training with a long list of new To Do's. And special thanks to Dixie Alcantar for always having my back, even when I push a little too hard to stay on the cutting edge as a market trend-setter. You are all a treasure and I love you.

Thanks to Heather Estay who helped me get all my crazy thoughts and words into this book, and for truly caring about me and having as much passion and dedication to the book as I did. I just adore you!!

A HUGE thank you to my six besties, the sisters we all chose to be sisters with — (in alphabetical order, so don't hate on me!) Gretchen G., Jennifer N., Raquel O., Ricci M., Tani M. & Tawnya E. Thank you taking me in when I was so very lonely in the foster home. You helped me realize we all had better lives in store in the future.

I would also like to thank those of you reading this book and who had the faith to pick it up and give it a shot. Please know that there is a better way of doing this business. Please know that you all have my lifelong commitment to strive for excellence and pass all my knowledge to you.

To your extraordinary success!

Krista Mashore

Table of Contents

Introduction

I do *not* rely on traditional measures of obtaining clients and generating leads. I will never do open houses, cold call or door knock again (unless the market dramatically changes, which I do not see happening). In fact, my business model is the exact opposite! My business model is changing the way real estate is being done and how agents are perceived because I generate and create massive amounts of momentum and value for my clients.

I operate differently because I am fighting against old school, traditional real estate agents who are *not* offering value to their clients. I know that, to be seen as a leader, to be relied upon, respected, trusted and valued, I have to give exceptional value! I have to do things differently. I have to be smarter! To be innovative! To use technology. I have to apply the principles like the Fortune 500 Companies do for their clients.

I offer a product and service that is *game changing.*

You may be thinking, "How does she do this? How is this even possible?"

If you ask old school real estate agents and traditional real estate coaches who are teaching and coaching because they themselves could not sell, they would tell you this is impossible and it will not work. Yet it's happening, every single day! It's happening through the art and science of what I call Socialized Marketing.

The fact that you've picked up this book tells me you are committed to success. It also says you are open to coaching and learning, and may be ready to become a Community Market Leader. Here's my definition of that term:

> "Domination of market share within a specific geographical location, accomplished by **excellence** in education - which really is marketing - innovation, technology and engagement. As market leaders, we pledge a solemn promise to our clients, and to ourselves, to give nothing other than one hundred percent in all we do with the utmost integrity."

Becoming a Community Market Leader

What's a Community Market Leader in real estate? You know this already. It's the person you think of and say, "Oh, she *owns* that market" or "He's got the pulse of everything happening." "She runs her business like a *business* not a hobby." "He's the one whose face you see all over town, the person whose name everybody seems to know." A Community Market Leader is the person who regularly ranks #1 in transactions in your community.

I'm that person in my community and I want to teach you how to become that person in yours.

I don't say this to brag, but to let you know that my success in dominating my location didn't happen by luck or accident. I'm smart and determined, but so are you. So, what do you need to do to get you into that Community Leader position? I'm going to show you.

First, let me be clear, I don't follow the same playbook that traditional real estate agents and brokers follow. I learned early on that if I wanted extraordinary results, I had to be different than the others. I had to come up with innovative ways of marketing and running my business. I had to eliminate traditional practices that *didn't* work (like holding open houses, cold calling, or door-knocking)

2

and *improve* traditional practices that *did*. For example, when I first started 16 years ago, I invested in high quality, full color, four-page brochures instead of flimsy, cheesy one-page flyers. Before the days of Zillow and individual real estate marketing sites, I put small CDs out as "virtual tours." I also marketed my listings on television. To stand out from the crowd, I had to stretch personally and professionally, see things from a different perspective, and push myself through any fear or self-doubt.

And you will have to do the same.

The reason I love continually learning is that I know there's a better, more effective way to do almost anything—even if you're already good at that thing. That's why I dive into situations that might stretch my thinking and challenge how I do things. Learning even one small thing each day allows me to keep expanding into the next "better way." More importantly, I implement that better way and continue to improve on it.

Basic Principles

Throughout this book, you're going to run into certain themes over and over again. These are basic principles I use in every aspect of my business. They aren't just a philosophy, they actually show up on a practical level in everything I do.

The first theme is to **go above and beyond** in everything you do and even in how you think. The question isn't, "Did I do enough?" It's always, "What more can I do? How much more value can I add to anything I touch or anyone I interact with?" That's how a Community Market Leader thinks and acts.

Another basic theme is **using technology**. I know, many of us get freaked out by technology and think it's beyond us. Years ago, I felt the same way. But the power of technology and the millions of ways you can use it make the effort to learn it totally worthwhile. Today, I use video emails to keep in contact with clients. I post market update videos on social media, and target market to a specific demographic and customer avatars. I have a digital marketing platform that is unbeatable and it changes monthly as technologies change. Of course, like you, I set up my digital lockboxes to track broker showings but the follow up I use is powered by my CRM (client relationship management) software. These are just a couple of examples. You'll see many more throughout this book. But keep in mind that *every* part of your business will be better when you get innovative with technology.

I also emphasize **being innovative**, doing whatever I'm doing in a way that's different than the way others do it. For example, I create educational videos about current topics and distribute them on multiple platforms to ensure maximum visibility. I design landing pages and use "cookies," which is a targeting system that monitors the behavior of online users, and re-targets and markets to them in the future. Being innovative involves using technology, but it's more than just technology. My lawn signs have solar lights so they show up at night and look nothing like any other in my community. We hand-deliver "Pick Your Neighbor" pieces (4-page full color brochures) to the surrounding neighborhood of our listings to ensure maximum engagement. I deliver a brochure to potential sellers *before* the listing appointment that tells them everything I do to market a home so that they are already sold on me before I walk through the door. I can go on and on about how I work to stand out and change things up based on what's happening in the market. Your thought needs to be, "How can I do this differently? How can I do this better than everyone else?"

Becoming an expert is another theme that is critical to my success and will be critical to yours. It's more than simply knowing how to fill out listing agreements or get into MLS. To be an expert in real estate you need to know your market inside and out. You need to be tracking economic and market trends to be on top of what's coming both locally and nationally. You need marketing and social media expertise to expose your client's home to the masses both locally and out of your area. As technologies change, you need to adjust your marketing plan to respond to how buyers search for homes and how sellers search for agents. This changes on a monthly, if not weekly, basis. You need to understand how laws and best practices can affect your buyer and seller. And, the only way you can do this is by educating yourself and researching to stay current.

The second part of being an expert is using that expertise to **educate others**, not only your clients but your general community. I'm not talking about throwing out a newsletter that cites a bunch of statistics nobody understands. A Community Market Leader uses his or her expertise to educate people. He'll send out brief videos that explain how different changes in the market affect sellers and buyers, both locally and nationally. She'll sit down with clients and make sure they understand how to get the best price for their home and walk them through the process step by step so they are totally clear about it. She doesn't take for granted what her client does or does not know. She dives deep into every aspect of the transaction from start to finish. She is intentional about what she is doing and she is relationship based, not robotic.

And by using this expertise effectively, you **build trust** with your clients and the broader community. Building trust is another basic principle and I'll show you the most effective ways to develop trust throughout this book. It's something that not only should be done, but it's an absolute *requirement*. Part of building trust is showing your community that you really know what you're doing. Another part of trust is being impeccably ethical in all you do, even if it means losing business. I *never* fudge the rules for a client or colleague for self-serving interests, and I *lead my clients* in a manner that will direct them to their best possible outcome, not mine. If something doesn't serve the client, if it doesn't serve the community, then it doesn't serve me. One of my mottos is, "Make good choices even when no one is looking and always have integrity." I say this to my children every morning, and if I forget to say it, they yell it over their shoulders as they run out the door. I incorporate that saying into my everyday life, both personally and professionally. You'll need to as well.

Which brings me to another basic principle that has played a big role in my success: approaching my work from **an attitude of service**. I want to give my clients and my community real value in everything I do. My focus isn't selling anybody anything. It's keeping my clients' best interests in the forefront, giving them everything they need and more than they expect. I don't show up saying, "Hey, look at me. I'm hot stuff." I show up saying, "How can I help you? "How can I be of service to you? How can I add value to you?"— and I mean it. This ends up translating into a ton of business coming my way. Just as important, it lets me sleep well at night! I approach my training and coaching business with this same attitude. I was put on this planet to serve, to be of service, and to give back. It's about how much I can *give*, not how much can I get. My saying is, "People before things. Take care of people and the things just come."

And if you do all of that—being totally trustworthy, becoming an expert and educating people with that knowledge, using technology, being innovative, always going above and beyond— you'll end up **being unique**, my last basic theme. To be a leader in any kind of business, you need to stand out from the crowd. You can't do things or think the way everybody else does. You need to step into your personal strengths rather than trying to be somebody else. If the top broker in your office is super-analytical, you can learn from that. But at the end of the day, if that isn't you, if you're more of an outgoing and enthusiastic person, emphasize those qualities. You'll get much farther for yourself and others by being *you* than trying to be someone you aren't.

I'm crazy hyper, fast paced, and energetic. You either love me or you hate me. I choose to associate with people and clients who appreciate my uniqueness, not those who want me to be someone else. I didn't feel this way at first. However, once I accepted myself for who I am, and focused on my strengths, my life and business became a lot more fun.

What You'll Get by Applying These Principles

As a Community Market Leader, you'll find yourself no longer chasing leads by holding open houses, cold calling or chasing expireds. Clients will seek you out. You'll be able to develop the kind of business that best suits you and your lifestyle. If you want to be #1 in your market, you'll have the skills to do it. If you want to spend more time with family, you'll be able to take your foot of the gas without destroying your credibility. If you want financial freedom, you'll be able to build it. Even if your goal is not to become #1, you'll be able to increase your business and have a more constant revenue with fewer ups and downs. Just imagine what you could do on your weekends if you didn't have to hold open houses or run out of town clients around. Rather than missing your kid's Little League games, ballet recitals, family BBQ's, and dates with your spouse, you'll actually have time to make a Sunday breakfast, have a lazy morning snuggling up with your partner or kids, or visit your parents and show them how much you appreciate them.

When you step into being a Community Market Leader, business gets easier because it becomes like clockwork. It just becomes part of who you are. As you start to gain market share, doing more business and making more money, you can hire good people—specialists in every part of the transaction— to help you.

Clients and others in the community will know and trust you. You'll be seen as a true professional. As a Community Market Leader, I continually educate myself so I'm abreast of what's happening. Whenever I walk into a presentation or meeting with a buyer or seller, I'm completely confident that my information is rock solid and my recommendations are backed by research. I know that what I offer is cutting edge in our industry.

I want you to feel that way too.

How to Use This Book

I'm going to cover a ton of information over the next several chapters. I'll teach you a bunch of specific tools and techniques I've used to create an amazingly successful business, tools that currently get me great results. And I'll show you how to stay on top of new tools. I'll give you some exercises and assignments to sharpen your skills, and I'll suggest resources to check out. And while it's great to read a book and gather information, the key is to *implement* what you learn. That's where the gold is.

Some people like to take it a step at a time, pausing after each chapter to put certain recommendations into place. If you're the kind of person who wants to read through the whole book, that's great. However, be sure to go back after you've finished reading and do the work. Definitely go back to the beginning and do it! Knowledge is just the booby prize if you don't put it into action.

Mastery, implementation, and consistency are so key. Be a *doer* not just a thinker. Apply the principles, master them, don't give up, be consistent. Have "definiteness of purpose." In Napoleon Hill's classic book, *Think and Grow Rich*, he writes, *"With the proper desire and definiteness of purpose, i.e. consistency and a 'never give up attitude,' you will end up succeeding."*

Will you need to do things differently than you've done them before? Absolutely! Will you go through a learning curve where you feel like a raw beginner again? Most likely. Will you need to step out of your comfort zone sometimes? Absolutely. Will you see results immediately? Maybe. But, by staying consistent and focused, you'll definitely see great results over time.

How do you swallow a whale? A bite at a time. Don't get yourself overwhelmed but take this in baby steps. If you just keep walking, anyone can climb Mt. Everest—not that I've tried, but you get my meaning. I didn't start out doing everything in my business the way I do it today. Over the years, I improved, innovated, tried some things that worked and others that didn't. I just kept going. Baby steps. I have spent hundreds of thousands of dollars —this is *not* an exaggeration—and thousands and thousands of hours learning and trying things that simply did not work. I've taken all the knowledge, training, trials, and errors and put them into a system that does work.

And I continue to sharpen and change my skills on a *continuous* basis as technologies change. I'm very clear that I need to consistently be innovative and stand out. As soon as my competitors start doing what I'm doing, I'm already on to the next idea and staying five steps ahead of the curve. This isn't done by luck or chance. It's done by constant education and focusing on what is relevant to what is happening now, and paying attention to what I foresee based on my research.

My goal is for you to be successful. I want you to be as successful as possible based on what you want out of this business. I'm going to give you the success strategies, the mindset, the approach, and the specific tools I use in my own business. As I'm writing this book, I've been in business for sixteen years. In my very first year, I closed sixty-nine transactions. And, since then, I've averaged one hundred transactions every single year for sixteen years running. I don't have a company of twenty brokers closing all those deals. That's me personally.

And that's not luck, my friends. That is not luck. It's following the principles above and applying those principles systematically in my business. It's never stopping and constantly improving. How exactly do I do that? Read on.

Take the Next Step

1. *Stop right now and pull out your calendar. Schedule enough time to read at least 10-15 pages of this book every day for the next few weeks.*

2. *Grab a stack of sticky notes. Whenever you run into a good thought or new idea, mark the page it's on so you can go back to it.*

Be sure to visit **www.sell100homesbook.com** for free resources that will help you grow and automate your real estate business.

CHAPTER ONE

Engage Your Community

In real estate, most of us have been trained to "sell ourselves" to attract clients. Well, I'm going to ask you to stop that. Just stop it! I'm going to ask you to "serve, don't sell." Business gurus call it "relationship marketing or content marketing" and it's used by many business giants you know, such as Nike, Apple, and Ikea. I call it engagement marketing because my focus is on engaging my community.

Do your research. This type of marketing is the new *new* of best practices. Before you know it, someone will come up with another best practice. My goal is to be the first in my area to adopt these best practices and apply them. It's your job too, if you want to have consistent income and clients flocking to you. A relationship is *not* built by sending out post cards or newsletters every month. You need to go much deeper than that to establish true connections and relationships and to engage people in your community.

In the good old days, agents used to hit the golf course, join a bunch of clubs, or show up to every community ice cream social and pancake breakfast to build relationships. That's okay, but honestly, who has time for all of that? And how many people can you meet personally and become buddies with? My practice of engagement marketing is nothing like that. This quote from Oracle Marketing Clouds' website is a good description:

> *"Relationship marketing is a strategy designed to foster customer loyalty, interaction and long-term engagement. It is designed to develop strong connections with customers by **providing them with information directly suited to their needs and interests** and by promoting open communication."*

Here's an even clearer explanation from Jay Baer, author of *Youtility*:

> *"What if businesses decided to inform, rather than promote? You know that expression 'If you give a man a fish, you feed him for a day; if you teach a man to fish, you feed him for a lifetime?' The same is true for marketing: If you sell something, you make a customer today; if you **help** someone, you make a customer for life. **In every business category, one company will commit to being the best teacher, and the most helpful**. And that company will be rewarded with attention, sales, loyalty and advocacy by consumers who are sick to death of being sold, sold, sold."*

As Community Market Leaders, we're going to engage people and build relationships by offering knowledge and service. And we're going to do it in a way that reaches zillions of people yet still has a personal touch.

I can say this because I've done it. When I show up to a listing appointment, people act like they've known me for years. Even if I've never met them, they see me as a good, trustworthy friend just because I've offered tons of information and service through social media and other marketing avenues. The client is fully engaged with me before I even open my mouth! (Wouldn't you rather show up to an appointment like that rather than sweating bullets about impressing a stranger?)

Here are four definitions of "engage" and how they relate to being a Community Market Leader: 1) *To occupy attention* (you get peoples' attention when you offer what they're interested in), 2) *To secure for employment or hire* (we definitely want them to engage us as their real estate professional, right?), 3) *To attract or hold fast* (when we offer expertise and service freely, our community is attracted and loyal to us), and, 4) *To bind, as by pledge, promise, or oath* (we give our promise to do our best for our community).

How the Big Guys Do It

It might surprise you to know that giving service and educating people while asking for nothing in return is a highly effective marketing strategy. You're marketing in a way that doesn't feel like you're pushing yourself on them. You're giving them value and they appreciate it, and appreciate you for giving it.

The majority of our most recognizable companies like Google, IBM, General Electric, Nike, Apple, and Whole Foods use this philosophy. They're educating the consumer and offering value rather than hammering at them. And they're creating enormous success with it! If it works for some of the best companies in the world, it's worth considering, right? So, what exactly do they do? Here are a few examples:

Whole Foods: Whole Foods does tons of education. They offer customers information on healthy living and eating. They give useful tips on how to eat inexpensively, and create articles on how to feel healthier based upon what you put into your body. In each store, they have Take Action Centers which, according to their website, "offer customers a wide variety of information on local, regional, national, and international issues of concern. Customers not only learn about important issues like genetic engineering, organic foods, pesticides, and sustainable agriculture, but we offer them the means to affect change by keeping them updated on new legislation and the tools they need to effectively participate in shaping those issues." How can you give value to your community similar to the value Whole Foods gives?

Ikea: Ikea is known as "the king of content marketing." Here's a quote from Ikea's president about their philosophy: "So, we really start with the customer, and try to see what's important to them... And then how can IKEA help them so that we are truly partners in making their life better at home every day." For example, check out their First:59 program. One of their surveys showed that 72% of people feel stressed on weekday mornings. So, Ikea created a whole website dedicated to tips on how to get your day off to a good start. Brilliant! Find what your community needs and give it to them. Figure out their pain points and fix their problems, just as Ikea does.

Moxie Pest Control: Moxie Pest Control designed an attractive "infographic" of a 7 Step process that shows you how to check your hotel room for bed bugs. (The first step is to leave your bags at the door in case you need to make a quick getaway!) How valuable is that, especially to frequent travelers? You can just print the guide out and throw it in your suitcase. With this graphic, Moxie not only shows off their expertise, but also gives us something valuable for free. Think of ways, even outside of real estate, that you can help your community and add value to them.

Lays: Lays (which is a Pepsi Cola brand) took a different approach. They got their consumers involved with a *Do Us A Flavor* campaign. They ran a contest with cash prizes for people to submit their ideas for new flavors for chips. Everyone who submitted an idea got a graphic of their idea on a bag of chips. Then Lays set up a Facebook page where people could vote on their favorite new flavors. The campaign was fun and got people involved and engaged.

What could you do? I did a challenge on Facebook: "I need your HELP Friends and Family.....$100 Visa Card to the person who can design my next Bill Board ad w/ a Catchy Slogan. Something memorable, like the ads we see for Chick-fil-A trying to tell people to Eat more Beef. Bring it on People!" I was shocked at the number of responses and, even better yet, the great ideas they came up with. The community actually designed my billboard ad and I recognized them for doing it. My new billboard "Krista, The Key to Sold" was brilliant!

That's the key to marketing, giving the community something they want and something that adds value to their lives. When you do this, you're marketing to them, though they don't really know it, and they certainly don't feel like they're "being sold." You're not asking your community for anything back. You're just giving them something. And, when you do that, you develop a relationship and they feel comfortable with your motives and confident with your service.

If you are ready to become "the best and most helpful teacher," you first need to become an expert at what you do.

Become an Expert

Many people get into real estate because they think it's easy—and it is. It's way too easy to get your license. For example, in California, you have to provide proof of completion for 135 hours of required education (45 credit hours in Real Estate Principles, 45 credit hours in Real Estate Practice course, and 45 credit hours in one additional state approved course). And, we all know that if you do the classes online, you'll spend much less time than 135 hours. Just pass the test (which is pretty simple). Bingo! You're now perfectly qualified to advise people and deal with them on what is probably the biggest investment they will ever make.

Really? In what universe? It takes over *500* hours to become a licensed *manicurist!* I can go on and on about the time it takes for other professionals to become licensed in their fields. So, why does it take so little time and effort to become a licensed real estate agent? Why don't we have mandates or requirements on how many homes you need to sell every year to maintain a license? (This is a topic that I could spend hours on.)

Or, maybe you have a little experience. You've done a couple of transactions, and worked under a more experienced broker. You've attended company seminars and even taken a couple of continuing education courses. I know you're sincere and want to do good work for your clients. But do you honestly think you've got the expertise you need to do a great job? Even if you've been in the business for twenty years, can you really call yourself an expert if you aren't staying on the leading edge of what's happening in real estate? Ask yourself: "How have I expanded, improved, and evolved in my business?" "Am I making strides to make it better?" "Am I still doing the same things that I learned when I first got into the business?"

Please don't compare yourself with the agents and brokers around you. You need to be different! If your goal is to be a Community Market Leader, you need to set your sights a lot higher. Everybody and their mother says they are an "expert" in real estate. Just go online and see how many agents claim to be experts—even after only four months in the business!

The truth is, our profession has a negative reputation. In the 2008 crash, there was so much fraudulent behavior going on in the real estate industry. Homes were appraised one hundred thousand dollars more from one month to the next in the same neighborhood. We had the mortgage crisis, our economy dropped, and the housing market crashed. Too many people experienced foreclosures, short sales, and bankruptcies. Everyone blamed Realtors®, lenders, and banking institutions, which is all real estate related.

So, we've got a negative image to overcome. Part of that negative image is that it's so easy to become a real estate agent. You don't need a lot of education, and it's not difficult at all to pass the test. We have people jumping into the industry who really have no business ever considering handling other people's most important assets. Everyone thinks it's an easy job and most agents treat it that way. They don't take it seriously. In turn, the community is not taking *you* seriously. We have to work harder than ever to establish trust, gain respect, and show we know what we're doing and will treat our clients fairly. I cannot tell you how many times I walk into clients' homes and they go on and on about what a poor past experience they've had. They are gun shy, to say the least. They dealt with an agent who just didn't have a clue as to what they were doing. That prior agent made errors that caused undue distress and loss of money, probably due to inexperience and lack of expertise.

Many agents, even when they reduce their commission, are making more money than they should because they're not doing their job correctly. They're not truly advocating for their seller or buyer. These agents are just getting by, doing the bare minimum. And people aren't stupid. They can see that. It's time to step it up, my friends, and treat your business like a business. Do you think McDonald's built their brand by flipping a few burgers then sitting back to wait for crowds of people to burst through their doors? No, they were intentional about their business and treated their business as a business.

The good news is that as soon as you actually run your business like a business, go above and beyond, and dive in to become an expert in this field, you automatically earn respect from people. It happens quickly because you stand out as being different and as a leader in your field. That is what this book is about. It's about being a leader and treating your most valued asset, your customer, as you should: like they are the most important person in the world and that without them, you would not be in business.

In his book, *Outliers*, Malcolm Gladwell claims that it takes 10,000 hours to become an expert. Think about it, that's around 10 hours a day for 1,000 days! Even if you have a lot of aptitude, Gladwell said in an interview, "The point is simply that natural ability requires a huge investment of time in order to be made manifest." The author of *So Good They Can't Ignore You*, Cal Newport, emphasizes that *how* you're using those 10,000 hours is equally important. He says you need to push yourself to the very limits of your current skillset to really expand into expertise.

Can we agree that standard continuing education and twenty transactions under your belt don't qualify you as an expert? In California, where I live, the average agent sells six homes per year. Within that average are the big dogs, like me, who are selling 150+ homes. That means everyone else is only selling five or six, right? Really, how can you master *any* profession if you only do it five or six times a year? You cannot!

Personally, I'm comfortable defining myself as an expert. I've worked in real estate for sixteen years. I've sold just under 2,000 homes, averaging 120 homes a year (though now it's more like twelve to fourteen a month). And even though I have all that experience, I still take a minimum of three to five webinar classes a week. Some of the classes help me track trends in real estate, business, or the economy. Others are about technology, marketing, and digital marketing so I stay on the cutting edge of marketing techniques. I push myself to take classes and read about whatever will enhance the value I can give to my clients. (I'll guide you to specific courses and credentials I've found valuable in the Resources section.)

I was heading to yet another out of town training a while back, and my dad said to me, "Why do you do all these trainings, Krista? You're already #1 in our area." I said, "Dad, the reason I'm #1 in the area is *because* I'm doing these trainings." I don't think he really got it. But, the point is, you can never stop learning. The second that you stop learning is the second you lose your claim to being an expert. The world is always changing and you need to keep up with those changes to be an expert. You also lose your place as #1 or as a Community Market Leader because somebody is going to come along and outshine you. This is true in any profession. Many parts of this book could apply to any entrepreneur, because the techniques and practices that I use are used by leading companies all over the world.

What does this all have to do with engaging your community? It has *everything* to do with it! You can be the nicest person in the world, but the person your community will flock to is the one who has the expertise. Ask yourself, when you go for surgery, are you looking for the nicest, most fun surgeon in town, or the one who clearly demonstrates his surgical expertise? Yeah, me too.

You first have to become an expert so you have valuable knowledge to share with your clients and community. That expertise includes knowing about the market, where it's going, and how current trends affect buyers and sellers. I spend an average of five to seven hours per week just learning and researching to keep current in our industry. I enjoy it. But, even if you don't, you should be spending at least an hour or two every week to keep up with what's happening.

I have to tell you that my father was one of the proof readers of this book. He highlighted this section and said that it's too much to tell people to take lots of classes and continuing educating, that they'll starve to death because they won't have time to actually make any money. I respectfully disagree. Once you stop learning and educating yourself, you stop growing. In the next few years, the market is going to change drastically. In my opinion, we are going to see two types of companies. One will be discount brokers who will offer little to no service and value, who will cut their commission. The other will be brokers that offer full service and value. These agents and brokers will go above and beyond, stand out, market, push, and charge a full commission. But the agents in the middle? I'm pretty sure they'll go to the wayside. I'm seeing it happen even now. When I meet with clients they have no problem paying me a full commission because they expect more and they see the value in what I'm offering. These clients realize that, in this day and age, if you're doing things the way you should be, you're keeping up with technology and using it effectively—and that's worth a full commission.

Because I was an educator, learning is in my nature so it's easy for me. If it's not easy for you, figure out a way to make it easy. Use audio downloads and audio books. Download Audible or another software. Listen to educational business and real estate books while you're getting ready for work or cooking dinner. That's what I do. I try to not waste any spare minute, even when I'm standing in line, or driving. It has helped me immensely.

What information is useful to share? Neighborhood information, market data, statistics, absorption rate, average days on market, list price and sales price, if the market trend is going up or down, if foot traffic per buyer is up or down, information on interest rates, any changes in the real estate market, or anything that's new, that's different. You want to let your community know what's happening both locally and nationally, and *especially* how it affects them personally. People don't care about you, they care about themselves and how they and their families will be affected positively or negatively.

For example, as I'm writing this book, we just had the PMI (private mortgage insurance) for FHA mortgages, drop from 0.86 to 0.6 percent. I created an informational video explaining how this would impact buyers. Average buyers are now going to save $2,000 per year on their PMI insurance. It's good information that is valuable people. Crazily enough, within a week of that drop in the PMI, the powers that be increased it again. That is how quickly our industry shifts. Most agents didn't even know that the rate had changed — how scary is that?

One great resource for this information is the National Association of REALTORS® (N.A.R). Check out the annual Home Buyer and Seller report. It explains the behavior patterns of a buyer and seller, and gives direct insight into how and what you should be marketing. This report is typically provided within your state's association. The statistics from the previous year come out in March of each year. If you aren't reading it, you're doing yourself and your clients a disservice. I don't mean to sound harsh but if agents aren't willing to do their jobs to this level, let's ask them to step aside so professionals who have the attitude and business practices of a true Community Market Leader can provide true expertise, service, and value to those they serve.

Other resources I use include Inman News, Digitalmarketer.com, and Content Marketing Institute for business trends, information on changes in the economy, updates, and cutting edge best practices in business. I also use Facebook groups like Lead Gen Scripts and Objections, Internet Marketing, Digital Marketing Institute, Community Market Leader, and The Paperless Agent.

Your Secret Weapon: Video

In the good old days, ambitious Realtors® would take their expertise out into the community by getting speaking engagements for local groups. They'd speak at their local Rotary Club, B to B forums, or Chamber of Commerce events. When email became popular, a lot of brokers started using email to blast out communications to their community.

While both of these methods are okay, a far more powerful tool—and the tool that I use—is video. It allows me to develop a relationship with my community and they grow to know, like, and trust me. People typically make a judgement about you within a few seconds, so video gives them a chance to get to know your personality before they actually meet you in person. A study from

Eric Wargo of the Association for Psychological Science titled, "How Many Seconds to a First Impression?" states that a first impression is actually formed in milliseconds.

According to Cisco, by 2017 video will account for 69% of all consumer internet traffic. Cisco also says, "It would take an individual more than 5 million years to watch the amount of video that will cross global IP networks each month in 2020. Every second, nearly a million minutes of video content will cross the network by 2020. [. . .] Globally, IP video traffic will be 82 percent of all consumer Internet traffic by 2020."

The world is using and watching a lot of video. Are you? Think about how many times you watch videos on Facebook, Instagram, or during internet searches. People watch video both for information and research, as well as for amusement and entertainment. Are you using video in your marketing practices? Are you using video to educate and add value? If you are, show your clients these statistics about video volume and explain how you can use it wisely on their behalf (see Chapter Three). Anything that you do, or do not do for that matter, should be based on research, statistics, and data. You can use what you are or are not doing, and *why*, when meeting with prospective clients.

If you're not yet using video, I encourage you to use it. As much as you might be afraid of the camera, as much as you might not feel comfortable at it, I am telling you that it's worth it. You don't need expert lighting or an Oscar-worthy script. You just need to take good information and present it in a way that is meaningful to people who may not know a lot about real estate. If you have a video camera, great! But you can also use the camera on your laptop or even on your phone.

Even after the hundreds of videos I've done, am I perfect? No. Do I make mistakes and stumble over words? Yes, all the time. Do I care? No! I'm human, right? And, the community doesn't care either. They want me, and they want you, to be human. In fact, I'll often post my bloopers. People love seeing them and it shows that I'm not a robot or perfect.

These days, when I do a video, I don't practice at all. But starting out, you may want to do a couple of run-throughs until you find your rhythm. If you feel self-conscious, take your focus off yourself. Focus instead on the people you're making this video for: What do they need to know? How can you explain it in a way they'll understand? How can you help them? How can you add value to them, serve them? Make a brief list of talking points you want to cover. Then, don't stress— just go out there and do it! If you do enough research and know your topic, you'll speak with confidence, and that's how you start to be recognized as a leader in your area.

I have always had a super fear of public speaking. My coach gave me some great advice. "Krista, don't make it about you. Make it about how you're helping people, and what they are going to get from your speaking. Think about how you are helping them, and how by speaking, you can change their lives for the better." This alone has helped me to step out of my shell and turn my nervousness into excitement. In her book, *The 5 Second Rule*, Mel Robbins writes about courage. She says that anytime you are nervous or have anxiety about anything, tell yourself that those nerves are truly excitement. Talk yourself out of nervousness and into excitement. It truly works!

This practice alone—making informational videos— has been a key factor in almost a thirty percent increase in my gross commission from 2015 to 2016. My GCI went from $1.3 million to $1.8 million. As time goes by, my business continues to multiply and grow, and I attribute a lot of that growth to these videos.

Your video should be brief, no more than one minute. If you can't cover everything you want to cover in that time, make a couple of videos as Parts 1 and 2. People are in a hurry and won't pay attention for much longer than a minute or so. New research suggests that shorter is better. You want viewers to be able to watch your video in-between other things they do (i.e. while waiting in line for their Starbucks). Later, you may want to create charts or graphs to illustrate what you're sharing.

Let me just warn you about something: When you're an expert in something, it's easy to forget what you *didn't know* when you first started. In other words, make sure that you're presenting your information in ways that people can understand. In writing this book and putting together my training courses, I've continually had to remind myself of that. I know how to be a Community Market Leader backwards and forwards. But, when I started teaching it, I realized I had to take fifteen steps back and start from the very beginning. I had to get a lot more specific about each piece and not just gloss over a technique or concept as if everybody already understood what I meant. (If they did, why would they bother learning from me?)

When I'm educating buyers and sellers about the real estate process, I take each and every aspect and break it down in layman's terms. We assume everyone knows how the real estate process works. Yet, the majority of people have no clue. They're scared and they need it to be broken down. I do the same in my informational videos. When people see how I break concepts down on the videos, they're more comfortable with me. They know that *I* know what I'm doing. I'm taking the time to walk them through it. Keep this in mind when you present information to your community. People are smart, but they don't know everything that you know. Explain whatever it is in a way that a non-expert could get it. Keep it simple and in laymen's terms, not real estate-speak. Real estate terms, procedures, and processes are commonplace to you, but not to a seller or buyer. They don't know what to expect or what "normal" is.

I recently recorded my listing presentation, totally spur of the moment and with no practice. I asked a colleague to act as a potential seller. Now I send that video before I go to a listing appointment. It saves me time and, more importantly, establishes me as the agent of choice. My closing ratio is around 93% for listings and that is rarely with any reduction in commission on my side. Why? The clients see the value in what I provide. Provide enough value and *show* the value you provide. If you do this, you will be unbeatable.

Don't use your videos to say, "Call me to sell your house." Instead begin with, "Here's something you might need help with or want to know." Then close with, "Please let me know what other videos I can do to help you. Let me know. I'm here to help." Don't be asking for the sale: "I'm great! Hire me!" Before you ever get to that point, you should give them a ton of value. Do that well and you won't even have to ask for the sale.

One of the huge benefits of sharing your expertise through video is just that—people get familiar with you and you don't have to sell yourself as much. When I go to a listing appointment, it's like the clients already know me. Even if I've never met them before, I've developed trust and a relationship with them through all the videos they've seen of me giving good information. I don't have to sell myself to them. I'm already sold.

To get to that point, you need to make sure that your informational videos show up *everywhere*.

Being Everywhere

Now, what do you do with those videos once you've started making them? Here are some statistics to consider: Cisco says that global internet traffic in 2020 will be 95 times more than the volume in 2005. Internet traffic will average 21 GB per person by 2020 versus 7 GB per capita in 2015. Google Analytics Hour of Day Report states, "Most websites receive the majority of their visits during the day when people are awake and have predictably busy periods during weekdays. You may see spikes in website traffic just before school or worktime in the morning (7am to 9am), or at lunchtime (12pm to 2pm), or right after school or work (4pm to 6pm)." Knowing this gives you a good clue about when you should be sending those video emails (BombBomb)!

The key is to use the power of the internet and post your videos in as many places as you can to get the most exposure. Of course, you'll post them on your website and email them to your client and prospect lists (paying attention to the times most people go online per Google Analytics). You also want to post them on Facebook, Instagram, LinkedIn, Twitter, and any new social media platform that comes along. I'm sure that by the time this book is published—and maybe before I finish this sentence!—someone will create the new *new* of social media platforms. You and I will be on that too.

My goal is to complete a new educational or market update video about two times per month. And, my team creates a property virtual tour video for every single house I list. All are distributed on numerous digital platforms. I also use search engine optimization (SEO), which we will get into in Chapter 3.

I have to tell you, everywhere I go in my community, people are always saying, "Hi, Krista!" to me. Half the time, I have no idea who they are. They think they know me because they see me so much on social media and other marketing vehicles. I act like I know them, too, "Hi, how you doing?" (My husband, Steve, asks, "Who is that?"' and I say, "I have absolutely no idea.") By creating videos, you become a celebrity in your area for your profession. You literally become the community real estate rock star!

I was getting my hair done the other day, and my hairdresser said, "The lady over there kept saying she knew you from somewhere." Apparently, the woman finally figured it out and told my hairdresser, "I know where I've seen her. I see her all over Facebook. I love her videos!" The woman lived in a town about 45 minutes away. I stopped by and talked to her and she said her family discusses the videos. She was really happy to meet me and said she felt like she already knew me. I am not exaggerating when I say that I literally have hundreds of stories like this.

Human connection is the key to personal and career success. I might never have run into that woman. Yet, through my videos, she had connected with me on a personal level. That's a part of the definition of engagement marketing: marketing that involves the creation and sharing of online material (such as videos, blogs, and social media posts) that does not explicitly promote a brand but is intended to stimulate interest in its products or services.

An article from Content Marketing Institute (http://contentmarketinginstitute.com/what-is-content-marketing/) states:

> *"Our annual research shows the vast majority of marketers are using content marketing. In fact, it is used by many prominent organizations in the world, including P&G, Microsoft, Cisco Systems, and John Deere. It's also developed and executed by small businesses and one-person shops around the globe. Why? Because it works. Specifically, there are three key reasons — and benefits — for enterprises who use content marketing:*
>
> - *Increased sales*
> - *Cost savings*
> - *Better customers who have more loyalty"*

Engagement marketing is a part of developing trust from your community. People will want to work with you because they like you and trust you even before they meet you face to face. You've given them a lot without asking for anything in return.

Now, if you're thinking that you can send out your information with a well-written email blast and get the same result, you can't. Think about your own experience: Compare learning by reading an email versus watching a video class online. Which one makes you feel most connected with the teacher?

Also, the statistics on open rates for email shows that it's declining. Here are a couple of graphs from Google analytics:

Open Rate Benchmark by Year

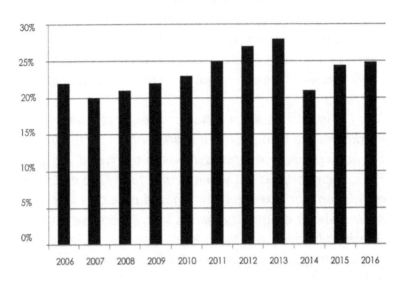

When you use email, you have to make sure your email is irresistible so it will get opened. One of the ways to make it irresistible is by creating a short video for whatever you want to communicate.

	Open Rate	Click-through Rate
Benelux	16%	20%
Denmark	31%	23%
Germany	25%	24%
Norway	18%	10%
Sweden	17%	12%
Switzerland	29%	18%
United Kingdom	13%	13%
Rest of the world	40%	5%

A lot of business people don't do engagement marketing and marketing through education because they think it takes too much time. And you know what? It might take a little more time than you're used to, especially in the beginning. However, with a little practice, the videos will become easier and you'll develop an efficient system to get them distributed. It's all worth it, because you're making a long-lasting impression.

As you continue to give value and educate people, offering them information they need to help them be more successful or to make an educated choice, your community will lock into you. Though it might take a little bit longer to do this process than running an ad in the local paper, it really pays off once you're established. You're not going to able to go anywhere without everyone knowing who you are. People are going to like you because you're giving them something they really want to know.

People call me now and say, "We see you everywhere. We want you to list our house." Recently, I hit the iPhone store thirty-five minutes away from my house. The young clerk there said, "Aren't you Krista Mashore? I've seen you everywhere and I especially love your videos. We're selling in four months, and my wife says we have to call you. She watches your videos all the time on Facebook." This sort of thing happens to me daily. I'm not trying to brag or say, "I'm so great." What I am saying is that I know what I am doing is *working*. Everyone knows a Realtor®. Many of my clients say they have many Realtor® friends. But they chose to call me because I am so knowledgeable, innovative, and different! Keep in mind that sellers and buyers typically start thinking of selling and buying 4-6 months prior to pulling the trigger. They research and gather information prior to making their choice. Help them choose you by standing out and giving them the information they need to make an educated decision.

On the same day I visited the iPhone store, I had an appointment with the Comcast guy at my house. He came in and said, "I see you

everywhere. I knew I was going to run into you one of these days."
Then he started talking to me about buying a house, and for twenty
minutes I just answered questions, giving him information and being
as helpful as I could.

Is he a hot prospect? No, he's not anywhere near ready to buy
yet. But I was helping him because that's what you do. It isn't about
me and what I can get from the interaction. It's about what value I
can give to everyone. And, in a few years when he's ready to buy,
you bet he'll call me. This happens frequently. Someone meets me
somewhere at a time when they weren't quite ready to buy or sell
a home. They remember me as helpful, rather than pushy, salesy, or
slick—and they keep seeing me all over the place so they don't forget
my name!

We treat every precious lead that comes in like gold. Whenever a
buyer contacts me through a site like Zillow or Trulia, we automatically
send them a buyer's guide through our CRM. When a seller makes
initial contact, we send them a seller's guide. These are not just the
cheesy, generic seller's or buyer's guides. These guides are current
and relevant, and changed every season to reflect market data and
trends. We give them information that is up-to-date and relevant
about current market stats, what's happening in the area, and how
that affects them in buying or selling. The seller's guide tells them
how long houses are staying on the market, what to do to get their
house ready, and why. Even if they don't become my client, I've given
them something of value and asked for nothing in return. (By now,
this theme should sound familiar!) We also send out a video thanking
them for contacting us and letting them know one of our associates
will contact them shortly to answer any questions they might have.
Then they are automatically put on a "Buyer's Drip" campaign.

The Buyers Drip campaign automatically reaches out to buyers
and keeps in constant contact. Often, buyers who aren't being
serviced properly will switch to an agent who is servicing them. We
have a company policy of a minimum of 7-9 touches. According to a

recent study, text messages are the best method of communication because 93% of all text messages get answered within five minutes. For example, we send a text letting them know we've sent them an e-mail with information they can use, or a text asking if there is anything we can do to assist them. Sending a video text message or video e-mail is an excellent way to develop rapport and make a connection. Stand out, be different, show effort!!

Another item I send to potential listings is ListReports, which is actually free. It gives them neighborhood demographics, nearby schools and the schools' scores, what restaurants are nearby, golf courses and parks, and how far they are from the home (www. ListReports.com). It's a great resource and has the exact address of the home, showing all of the above in relation to that specific property. Showing up to a listing appointment with this one piece of information alone will make you stand out from the rest.

Engage in Innovative Ways

There's a saying that says, "The more that you give, the more you receive." In Acts 20:35, the Bible refers to the fact that there is more happiness in giving than in receiving. I completely agree and believe that. My goal is to give as much as I can, not because I'm going to get business in return. I know it will come because that's how the universe works, right? What goes around comes around? Every action generates a reaction. So, we're going to keep our focus on giving value and doing it in a way that's *innovative*. I speak this always and often use it in my signature line: "People before things.... The more value you give, the more you'll receive."

I was a third-grade teacher for six years and I talked really fast. My students would just sit there with their jaws dropping because I had so much energy. I had their complete attention because if they stopped looking even for a second, they wouldn't be able to keep up. They learned quickly how to follow along with me.

But I really got them engaged when I got innovative. For example, I love to cook, so every Friday I'd cook with the class. I'd relate cooking to life and whatever we were studying. If we were doing math and fractions, we'd make pizzas. I'd say, "Okay, let's cut the pizza in half. So, this is one half." Then I'd ask them, "Now how would you cut this pizza so that four people could eat it?" Instead of just showing fractions on the board, we cut up pizza. They got the concepts quickly and remembered them. Of course, making the pizza and eating it was fun, too.

This is adding value and being unique. I still see students from 20 years ago who still call me Mrs. Miller (my former name) and tell me I was their favorite teacher ever. The point is that I was unique, cared immensely about them and was diligent in trying to be the best teacher I could be for them.

I also had them listen to opera. Honestly, at first most of them hated it. They were used to *Barney* or *Dora the Explorer* or *Beevis and Butthead,* and here I was playing *Phantom of the Opera.* That said, because the music was so different, it caught their attention. They learned to love it, and they started asking, "Hey, can we listen to opera?" When I see those kids now, they tell me, "I still love listening to Phantom of the Opera." That just makes me smile. I made a difference twenty years ago to a bunch of eight-year-olds who still remember it to this day.

A lot of agents send out information that is somewhat valuable, but it's boring. They send articles on how to clean your gutters, tips on gardening, how to save energy, tips for refinancing, or recipes. I do that as well, but I do it on steroids. Instead of just emailing a newsletter with tips for sellers, I create a video on: "Hey, when you're selling your house, here's exactly what you should do!" The video is relatable and memorable, and I explain why they should do the things I recommend. I always show them the research behind it. For example, "If you fully stage your house, statistics show that you're going to make three to six percent more than if you don't." Instead of sending out a recipe card, I created a website and Facebook page called East County Fun where I review local restaurants and attractions of the community. Then I pay for advertising on social media platforms to plug those attractions and restaurants. This not only helps the businesses, it also benefits the community and me.

I've also created a number of landing pages. A landing page is not an extension of your website. It is created to capture someone's contact information by giving something of value. For example, I have a landing page that is titled "Home prices in Deer Ridge subdivision have increased seven percent in the past six months. Find out why." It's a very specific piece of information that will be valuable to homeowners in that area, or buyers interested in that specific community.

Years ago, I ran into some software that you can put on your website to determine the value of a home. Using that software, I created a landing page of "What's your home worth?" At the time, no one had done it so I got a ton of leads by providing potential sellers a good tool to find out the value of their home. After a while, agents in my area started copying me. Though I still use the calculator, I had to switch to something different.

I've made landing pages for first-time buyers, such as, "Know what you need to prepare to qualify for a mortgage" and "Five most common mistakes buyers make when purchasing a house." On these pages, I add in a mortgage calculator. For sellers, I've done pages like, "The seven most critical errors that sellers make that takes thousands of dollars from their bottom line." This page uses the home value calculator, but it first attracts potential sellers because they think, "Wow, I don't want to lose thousands of dollars. What should I make sure I don't do?"

For each landing page, I give people something of value. In exchange, I get their phone number and email address (in order to get what I offer, they have to input their contact information). Once I have their information, I don't just let it go. I set them up in my marketing campaign. I put them on an automatic drip campaign where they are constantly getting updates from me, information, and value. I am not asking them for anything, I am always giving.

By continually being innovative, you're not only standing out from the crowd, which in itself is a huge benefit. You are also showing the community that you care, you work hard, and you are different.

Innovation is about creating solutions for people in your community. You are intelligent, you have ideas, you're creative, and you have a vision, right? That is all you need to be innovative. How you engage your community will probably look very different than what you're doing now, but it's going to work for you. Research what big businesses are doing. Go to content marketing websites and digital marketing websites. Implement and tweak what they are doing. And do it early, before anyone else in your community is doing it. Being an early adopter is key.

Think again about the example of Ikea. They figured out areas where consumers needed help (less stressful mornings) and they put together a website to address the issue. What problems need solutions in your community? As I am writing this, we are having massive rain storms in Northern California. Currently, homeowners around here could use information on preparing for power outages, keeping their garages from flooding, handling downed trees, and shifting water away from their houses—anything storm-related. What solutions would be timely and valuable to your community? Put those on a webinar, landing page, or in a video.

Whatever you do, do it differently, offering as much value as possible. If you sponsor a community event, don't show up with tacky pens and flyers promoting how great you are. Show up with calendars of upcoming fun events, city sports team schedules (in my area Raiders, 49'ers, A's, Giants), or a contact list of places to volunteer in the community. If you organize a food drive, how about doing it in the summer rather than the holidays when everyone else does theirs? Maybe you can collect the extra vegetables and fruit people have in their own gardens rather than asking for cans. Or, you can set up a competition between schools, giving a prize to whichever school collects the most food. One super popular theme day that I created for my community was, "Vision Board Making Day." I created a video showing what a vision board is and why it's so important. Then, I invited the entire community to come to my office and make their vision boards with me. Lots of people showed up and everyone just loved it. Even better, I was able to help participants see a roadmap of their goals and add value to them.

Whatever you do in your community—Santa Claus visits, donating to schools, reaching out to teens—offer value and be innovative as you do it.

I've been fortunate enough to make a very good living so I can give back. I've created several events that give the proceeds to a child with cancer, or donate money to a family who lost a child. For example, here is the post I used for the "Amazing Race" event I created:

Krista Vitale Mashore shared Olivia's Story's event.
February 24, 2016 at 5:52pm · 🌐 ▾

HELP OLIVIA FIGHT CANCER!
Sign up for the
AMAZING RACE
3-12-16
East County FUN
What's Hot, New & To Do
www.EastCountyFun.com

| MAR 12 | **East County's Amazing Race** Sat 10 AM · 7620 Balfour Rd Brentwood, CA 94513 20 people interested · 22 people going | ✓ Going ▾ |

I am at the point in my life where I want to be more *intentional* about giving back. Everything in my studies and research emphasizes giving as much as I can to clients and people around me—and not letting my fear of people stand in the way of helping and adding value. In *Think and Grow Rich*, Napoleon Hill wrote that, while reading his book, you'll get an idea. He said that when it comes up, grasp it, go for it, and be intentional about implementing your idea. In one part, he noted that if kids in schools were forced to read his book, it would cut down their learning time by half. He thought it should be mandatory to read the book prior to graduating high school.

Immediately, a green light went off in my head. I was getting ready for work and listening to the audio book of *Think and Grow Rich.* I immediately stopped what I was doing, went to the computer, and typed out my idea. It was the seed idea of the program I created called *Teens Lifting Lives.* Here's what I wrote on a Facebook post (I also created a video):

> *$1,000 for TWENTY Young Minds Ages of 15 to 19 who live in Brentwood, Oakley, Antioch, or Discovery Bay who will read the book (or Audio Book) Think & Grow Rich from Napoleon Hill & be willing to commit to the Following for the next 8 weeks: If you are reading this please share.*
>
> *Here are the details and requirements:*
>
> *p.s. this is a drug and alcohol free program. I know that students from time to time may dabble in this; however, the commitment is that each student must take an oath and abide by it that they will keep 100% free of drugs and alcohol during this 8-week program and not be afraid to take a stand and voice their stance of being "Drug and Alcohol FREE" to those around them, even when being tempted or having peer pressure.*

1. *Will Read One Chapter each week, No More No Less and apply the skills and methodologies that he suggests.*

2. *Have a willingness to have an Open Mind and Desire to want to better yourself and add Value to others.*

3. *Will spend 25% of the $1,000 by Paying it Forward to ANY cause that will make a difference in the life of someone else. (You'll need to think about this and let me know in your application)*

4. *Promise to be a person in the community, whether it be at school or home, that has a standard of excellence in how they treat others (no bullies here, if you are a bully or gossiper, you'll have to stop for the 8 weeks, this is imperative).*

5. *If Chosen: Join the Facebook Group w/ the other 19 participants and give your feedback, support, and commitment to the other members in the Face Book Group for the 8 weeks.*

6. *Be willing to Earn the $1,000 by doing the homework that will be required each week (no more than two hours). This is dedicated to time of learning the book and applying the principles of Personal Growth and Development for oneself and the community (your efforts will be evaluated, if the effort is not put in we will be giving your $1,000 to the charity of your choice).*

7. *Meet every Tuesday via zoom video from 6:00-7:00 a.m. to review the book and share experiences*

8. *Have one full day of no social media or phone each week.*

9. *No social media, internet, or phone for 1 hour each day.*

10. *Meet for four hours to do goal setting w/ the group prior to the session starting.*

11. *Join in a Graduation Ceremony at the end where you will tell the members in the group and their families how reading the book has changed you and make a Vision Board*

Hint Hint, Reading Chapter 2 will help you in getting chosen. Definiteness of Purpose and having the Desire to Possess it will help you get chosen.*

*** Please apply by sending your application to Krista@ KristaHomes.com*** Applications are due Monday February 13th and the program will start on Wednesday February 15th. You will be notified if you made it on Monday February 13th. ***

There may be 2-3 times the group will meet for an hour together to master mind and share.

Please only apply if you are serious and dedicated to 8 weeks of improving yourself and others that surround you. Please apply only if you will commit to making a difference in yourself and others. This is NOT about making the money, but about making a difference.

I am dedicated to running this Program every 10 Weeks, so if you do not make it in the first round, you'll get another opportunity. My hope is that by my adding value to you, you will in turn add value to those around you!!

Application Requirements:

1. *Desire: Clearly define your desire. Exactly WHY do you want to be in the program? How will it help you and others? Visualize this and see yourself here.*

2. *Explain exactly what you will give in return for being in the program and who/what you will give the 25% of your money to. ($250 of the $1,000)*

3. *Explain how you Plan on making the time to read/listen to one chapter a week and apply the principles without it affecting your school.*

4. *Pledge to be 100% committed to this and your cause in writing.*

5. One and only one letter of recommendation as to why you would be great for this. Remember, you don't have to be a model citizen. If you are struggling with something and feel this class will help you, please apply. This is not just for the perfect students in the world, lol. It's for everyone (hey, when I was young I was actually in juvenile hall, so we all can change!).

***Only the first 50 Applications will be looked at. Please keep your application down to one page. (Please type it, it will make it easier on me. lol)

Good Luck Kids! Let's make a difference together!!!

Please email your applications to: Krista@KristaHomes.com

Sincerely,

Krista

I'm committed to taking on 20 students every ten weeks for the rest of my life. This program has been a lot of work but it's so fulfilling. I get a kick out of it, and the impact the program is making on the kids is amazing. Not for one second did I say or think, "I'm going to do this for business." It was purely to give and serve. However, you can't imagine all the buzz I've gotten from it. I even tried to take down my work information from popping up when I posted it. But Facebook insists on adding my links when my name shows up since I'm on the internet so much.

My point is that I created this program to help, to serve, to give back. In turn, it's helping me both personally and professionally. I am grateful to these kids for allowing me to experience such joy and fulfillment. To see how these young people grow and change over the ten weeks is even more rewarding.

Staying in Touch

According to a 2017 NAR report, 78% of buyers and sellers said they would re-use their agent—but only 24% of them actually did re-use their agent. Where is the disconnect?

HOME SELLING AND REAL ESTATE PROFESSIONALS

Exhibit 7-1
METHOD USED TO FIND REAL ESTATE AGENT
(Percentage Distribution)

	All Sellers	AGE OF HOME BUYER				
		35 and younger	36 to 50	51 to 60	61 to 69	70 to 90
Referred by (or is) a friend, neighbor or relative	42%	44%	44%	45%	43%	33%
Used agent previously to buy or sell a home	24	26	22	24	23	24
Internet website (without a specific reference	4	6	5	4	3	2
Personal contact by agent (telephone, email, etc.)	4	3	3	4	3	9
Referred by another real estate or broker	4	4	3	2	4	6
Visited an open house and met agent	3	1	4	2	2	4
Saw contact information on For Sale/Open House sign	3	3	4	2	2	3
Referred through employer or relocation company	3	3	7	3	1	1
Direct mail (newsletter, flyer, postcard, etc.)	1	2	1	1	1	3
Walked into or called office and agent was on duty	1	1	1	1	1	5
Newspaper, Yellow pages or home book ad	1	*	*	1	3	1
Advertising specialty (calendar, magnet, etc.)	1	1	*	*	2	2
Crowdsourcing through social media/knew the person through social media	*	*	*	*	*	*
Saw the person's social media page without a connection	*	*	*	*	*	*
Other	9	6	6	11	12	7

We have this amazing pool of potential clients in past clients. Yet, too many agents "love 'em and leave 'em." They may send out a Christmas card or a refrigerator magnet every year, but that's about it. Worse yet, they don't do anything at all. To be quite real, in the first ten years of my business, I wasn't very good about keeping track of past clients and following up. Now I know that prior clients are assets that are way too precious to be treated like yesterday's newspaper! Not following up back then cost me a lot of business. Today, I encourage you, even if you're just starting, to have a database of clients and continue to reach out to those people.

My father owns a company in Tahoe, NV called Second Home Care. He told me that if his clients didn't get an update from him a minimum of once per month about their specific home and the maintenance his company performed for them, his company would lose thousands of dollars every year. The bottom line is that people want communication. They want a personal touch. Think about staying in contact with current or past clients from your own perspective. How many times have you worked with a particular tradesman or been told to try out a specific restaurant? You have every intention to use the tradesman again or go to the restaurant, but "out of sight out of mind." It's so easy to forget people who've done good work or the things we mean to try if it isn't constantly in our faces.

I keep in contact with my previous clients *forever*. Obviously, by now, I have a ton of prior clients and there's no way I can follow up manually. Everything is automated (I use Realvolve), so no one slips through the cracks. I touch base with my clients several times throughout the year in different ways. Again, the key is offering value to them, not just, "Hi, remember me? I'm still selling houses!" Keep in mind, staying in touch does not have to be expensive! I'm doing well enough now that I can spend $2,000 on an annual party—but, that wasn't always the case. Be creative. Be innovative. Be different and give value.

Here are some of the ways I stay connected to my client base:

Every six months after closing on a property, we drop off a comparative market analysis (CMA), giving my past clients the specific comparable properties that have sold in their neighborhood. They remember me because I took the initiative to keep them updated about the value of their home and acknowledged their 6-month anniversary.

Let's talk about the holidays, the time when most of us think about reaching out. Everyone hosts Christmas holiday parties for clients, so I chose Thanksgiving instead. I have a pie giveaway around Thanksgiving where I also give wine. I hold the event at a local bar, which is pretty inexpensive. They give me the room for free and I pay for the alcohol. It's around $2,000 for the event, and about one hundred people show up. I give them a pie and get to spend quality time with them. The clients are happy to get the pie and they enjoy themselves at the event.

Around Christmas, I host a fun canned food event that includes the kids. Everyone is encouraged to bring canned goods or a toy for specific non-profits in the area. Santa comes and we have pictures with Santa for free, along with face painting, a balloon maker and a jumpy house. We serve hot chocolate and cookies.

Instead of Christmas cards or emails, I do a blast text message wishing everyone Happy Holidays. I do this because a) Christmas cards get lost in the shuffle and aren't very personal and b) the number of people who actually open their email is significantly less than the number of people who open their text messages. Ninety-three percent of all text messages get opened within five minutes.

Also, once per year I have a client appreciation party where I serve food, have games, and give prizes. I invite my past clients so I can say, "Thank you for allowing me to help you." We set up fake casino gambling where each person wins a prize. I personally cook all the food. (I know I'm crazy, but I love to cook and they love my food. They appreciate me even more for taking the time to cook rather than calling in a caterer.) Each year the party gets bigger and bigger and I try to outshine the previous year. I just recently closed two transactions from one of my past client's friends who had come to this event as guests for several years. Those two sales alone will cover the cost of the party for the next three years.

At minimum, every quarter you could send a BombBomb video email where you say, "Hey, just thinking about you." It can be one generic video, yet when you put their name in the greeting, it seems as if it was made just for them. During a transaction, I send my clients updates once a week, and once every other week I make a video update to tell them what's going on with the property. When a transaction is over, I send a thank you video and ask for a testimonial—much more powerful than asking for a testimonial by plain email.

I use the BombBomb videos in a multitude of ways. I have generic Happy Anniversary and Happy Birthday videos. I send a video on the anniversary of their sale or purchase. I send updates on the market. I try to stay in front of my clients as much as possible in ways they'll appreciate. But here's the key: Whatever you choose to do, do it consistently. **If you plan to just do something once and not ever again, don't bother doing it at all**.

Take the Next Step

1. Next time you're online, take a moment to visit the website of one of the Big Guys I mentioned. How do they position themselves? Do you feel like they are serving you or selling you? How could you apply this to your business?

2. Take a few minutes to think about your level of expertise in this business. Where are you strong? Where could you improve? How could you become stronger in your weak areas?

3. Pull out your phone. Make a video NOW. Send it to your spouse or your mom, but just take the plunge and do it.

4. Who are the people that are everywhere in your community? Maybe they're in real estate or maybe not. Where do you see them? What is your impression of them?

5. Brainstorm 5 new ways you could engage your community. Be innovative and think outside of the box. As you brainstorm, don't critique yourself. Even really lame ideas can lead you to a great idea.

6. Brainstorm 5 ways you can stay in touch with your circle of influence. Implement at least one of those ideas.

Be sure to visit **www.sell100homesbook.com** for free resources that will help you grow and automate your real estate business.

CHAPTER TWO

Create Your Unique Business

I want to clear up a huge misunderstanding that many agents have: You are *not* an employee. You're a business owner.

I see people starting out in this business and they try to "fit in" and follow in the footsteps of Realtors® around them. They act as if they've been given a job description with certain duties: hold open houses, cold call, door knock, work weekends and nights, and answer their cell phone 24/7. To be successful, they assume they can't choose what hours to work. The "job" drives their schedule. They don't think they can choose what clients to have or what their business looks like.

I get it. I did all those things. I even knocked on doors looking for leads, which took hours and hours away from my two little girls. When I started, I was a single mom with two kids ages three and five and a half at home. I had been married for six years, and had been a very successful credentialed third-grade teacher. I left my teaching career and jumped into real estate full-time. This was a risk and took total courage. Most great things in life won't come unless you find the courage to take a jump in a new direction and take action. Imagine, after going through school for years, getting my Master's Degree in Curriculum and Instruction so that I could become a principal, I just up and left my profession to go into a totally different line of work. It took some guts, to say the least. Was I scared? Of course. Did I have to overcome obstacles? Yes.

One thing I've learned over the years is that, if you really want to start a business and succeed you need a strong motivation. You need to be absolutely, totally clear about why you want this. Let me just share what got me launched on this path.

It started on a Saturday afternoon. I was at breakfast with five of my girlfriends and all our kids. We had all gone to high school together and our children were growing up together. We were having a great time, laughing, reminiscing, with the kids all running around. It was like your perfect Saturday morning. My phone rang and, being a brand new real estate agent at the time, of course I answered it. A friend of mine from college was on the other end and she told me she had just seen my husband in Napa. I said, "Oh yes. He's there at a golf thing for work." She paused then said, "No Krista, I'm so sorry but, I saw him being intimate with another woman Krista."

My heart started racing and I could feel my face flush. Tears instantly welled up in my eyes. I was hit with hurt and anger and an instant, crazy loop in my head: "But, we have kids. We built this life together. How many more lies did he tell? I just left my safe, full-time teaching job. How could he be so foolish to throw this all away?"

I remember driving home from the restaurant, doing my best to hold back the tears. Before I could even really wrap my mind around what was going on, I knew I was going to have to save myself. More importantly, I knew I was going to have to take care of my daughters and give them the life they deserved. I didn't know what that was going to look like. I didn't know how it was going to show up, but I remember a little voice saying, "Your world is about to change drastically, and you need to be ready for it."

In just a few moments, my world was gone, and I was at risk of losing everything. I panicked thinking I might lose my daughters, or they might not be able to live with me.

I was freaked thinking my kids could lose their home, that they'd lose any semblance of normalcy being thrown back and forth between me and their dad. My life got so crazy.

Within a week of my husband leaving me and tearing up what I thought was our happy home (I guess we all think that right before our world is torn apart!), I watched my two daughters being picked up from school by the new girlfriend who was driving my car! I mean who can even make up such craziness? Well, in a matter of days, this was my life. My why hit me like a ton of bricks: I needed to be able to support myself and my kids and give us a real life. My mission was to keep my kids in their home and to create as much normalcy as I could.

That vision and that why propelled me into becoming the rookie of the year in my first year in real estate. It got me to work smart and hard, selling 69 homes my first year and averaging at least one hundred homes a year thereafter. My daughters and living in survival mode was the motivation that built my business and put me in the top 1% of all Realtors in the nation.

Why do I tell you this? Why am I telling you my devastating and quite frankly embarrassing story? Because I want you to see and realize that we are all the same.

We are all made from the same thread. There is nothing special about me. I just made a conscious, consistent decision to move on, to fight and not let that devastating experience define me and the outcome of my new family, just my girls and me.

I didn't know it at the time, but the Universe (call it God, a higher power, whatever) had something bigger in store for me. When I left my teaching career abruptly to dive into a new career, it felt very daring and scary. The crazy part about this story is that if I hadn't taken that leap of faith, if I had let my fear of change get in my way, I would be in an incredibly different place today. On a teacher's salary, I never could have afforded to keep my children in the home they had been raised in. One of my main objectives was to protect my daughters, keep their environment as stable as possible. Looking back, I'm so glad that when I had the inclination to change careers and dive in, that I did it!

Because of my success today, people seem to think that it's all been smooth sailing. It hasn't. And, I didn't get to where I am just because I'm cute and smart—honestly, I've heard people say that! The reason I've been in the Top 1% is because I have an incredible work ethic, drive for excellence, strong appetite for educating myself, and I'm different. I've always approached this career as a serious business owner, even in the beginning when I was frightened and insecure.

You've got to start thinking like an entrepreneur, a business owner.

It's true that you don't have quite as many choices when you're first starting. When I began, I focused on buyers and did a lot of the traditional things like open houses to get leads. But, even back then, I was thinking like an entrepreneur, not an employee. I tried to do things a little differently than people in my office. I analyzed what was working and what wasn't. I knew that I was the one who had to create the kind of business and success I wanted. I constantly took classes to learn. I tried different things and failed, then failed again.

Don't get me wrong. My results were outstanding in my first year. But I wasn't as innovative then as I am now. I worked like crazy but I was timid about standing out and making myself known. I wish I had understood the awesome power of being bold and innovative. If you're new in real estate, you don't have to make that same mistake. Jump into this business *boldly*. Make a difference, and be different. Create your unique business and do the things your colleagues are not doing. Research what Fortune 500 companies are doing and find out ways to implement their techniques and strategies in your own business. Don't let your company team you up with, or have you follow around, the person who has been in the industry forever who does things just like everyone else. Be an entrepreneur.

Hire a coach. This may seem crazy to you, but I've been in the Top 1% nationally for sixteen consecutive years running, and I have a coach. I'll talk about this again in Chapter 5. But, for now, just know that it is difficult to do something new and be the best of the best on your own. You may need mentoring, constant pushing and help at implementing all you need to do to be the best, stand out, and make it happen! Don't be a lemming. Don't just follow the leader. Be the leader!!

My goal was always to be #1 in the market. Even in the beginning, I'd study the super successful brokers and figure out what I could do to be as successful as they were. I kept the techniques or approaches that fit me and discarded the rest. I started studying other businesses outside of real estate to see what made them successful. Then, I took what I learned and applied it to my business. For example, early on, I realized that I wanted more control over my time, which meant dealing with sellers rather than buyers. So, I turned my attention toward making that happen.

The point is that I didn't just drift along "doing real estate." Get a vision—which might change from time to time—of the type of business you really want. Then focus on putting that business together.

Your goal may not be to become #1. You may just want more revenue stability or to work with a different type of client. You may want a business that secures your financial freedom, or one that lets you control your time more. Whatever it is, the principles I'm sharing will help you get there.

But you need to start with your unique vision of what kind of business you want, then design your brand around that.

Developing Your Brand

Okay, you've probably worked with branding and might be thinking, "Hey, I can skip this section." Don't. Your brand isn't just some slick slogan you throw on your flyers. It's not just some spiffy logo or the angle du jour that's supposed to attract hot prospects. It's not just the colors you choose for your website. Your brand can't be some hollow strawman of what you think will sell or who you think people want you to be.

To be effective, your brand has to sincerely reflect what you're about. It needs to set you apart from the crowd and make you *unforgettable*. Your brand should be in the very DNA of everything about your business, from your business cards to the way you treat your clients to the way you market a listing. It's even in the clothes you wear. That means, if you're heading to Starbucks Monday through Friday, nine to five, you need to be in the type of business attire that reflects your brand.

Here's the thing: When you start applying the techniques in this book —the technology, community building, and innovation—you'll start getting massive exposure. You don't want an outdated brand and image blasting out to the community. You need to make sure that everything, from your photo to your website, reflects the business you are creating. As you adopt and implement the methodologies in this book, you'll get much busier. So, now is the time to get your brand right and start out on the right foot.

To find your unique brand, ask yourself a series of questions: "What is the vision I have for my business? How am I unique? What are my real strengths? How does my market perceive me now and how would I like them to perceive me in the future? What would I like people in my community to say when they tell someone else about me?"

How do you want people to *feel* about you and your brand? When they see your sign, and when they see your videos, how do you want them to *feel?* For example, when people see my materials, I want them to feel, "I trust her. I like her. She's real and approachable." Feelings are a huge part of marketing.

People are all over social media nowadays. They want to see anything and everything about you. They look on your social media pages. They see what you're doing. They see what you're interested in. Everything that shows up on your Instagram, Twitter, Snapchat, your LinkedIn, and Facebook pages is being watched. They're interviewing you on social media even when you don't have a clue that they're interviewing you.

Part of your brand is this personal side. People want to get to know you and form a relationship. I love to cook, I love to boat, I love to be on the Delta, and I love entertaining. I show that on my Instagram and my Facebook feeds. I *don't* post anything on those sites that I wouldn't want the world to know or see. I wouldn't post anything that would be detrimental to my brand.

Part of your brand is your personality. I've learned that I don't need to reach the whole world. I only try to reach the people who will connect with me, the people who realize the value of my kind of person. Don't be afraid to be who you are.

As for me, I have tons of energy. I talk fast and think fast. That's just who I am. I can be like a chameleon and slow down when I need to. But, for the most part, my clients love my fast pace. They know I'm going to work quickly in my business and I'm going to get results for them without dragging my feet. Even though I'm fast paced, I still treat my clients like dear, special friends. I take my time with them. I talk *with* my clients, not at them or to them.

I've also worked hard to become very professional at what I do and I enjoy working with clients who have done the same. I have a lot of education and work well with others who appreciate learning. I also love fun and humor, and I can be crazy at times. I have a degree in psychology and a Master's degree in curriculum and instruction. I'm a professional so I show up in a professional business suit, but I'm also going to hug my clients, give them a fist bump or a high five, depending on who I'm dealing with. I am a leader, not a follower.

I am, and will continue to be, one of those "early adopters" of the latest technology.

As you think about who you really are, also think about what type of client you want to attract. Who do you want to work with? I want to attract people who respect me both personally and professionally. If someone gets upset that I only see clients in the evening, one night per week (and I try to avoid even one night when possible), then they aren't the clients I want. I've learned the hard way that clients who are the most difficult in the beginning will continue to be that way. They'll demand every ounce of my attention, have little or no regard to my family time, and call at all hours of the night and on weekends. They are showing that they do not respect me, and they are not like me. I respect the professionals I work with and I also require mutual respect. I have boundaries and I respect other peoples' boundaries. These are the clients I want to attract.

This is important: Be who you want to attract, attract who you want to be. Don't scramble to reach the masses, reach the people you want to work with. Less is more and more is less, simpler is sweeter.

Your job as a Community Market Leader is to develop lasting relationships with people. Your brand does that. It introduces you to people and forms a relationship before you ever meet face to face. When I make educational videos, I show that I have a lot of knowledge and that I'm well-educated. Then I add my bloopers at the end. People get to see my crazy, funny side. They know I'm human. They learn to trust me because I'm giving them value without asking for anything in return, and they like me because I'm a human being, just like them. All of this is part of my brand.

Part of my personality is being positive and it's something I value. I show up with a smile and enthusiasm every day. I don't freak out when something unexpected happens but accept it and move on. Am I always feeling like that? No. Am I human? Yes. Do I have bad days? Yes. But I work to shift a negative mindset quickly, and show up with a positive attitude. People respond positively to positivity.

By the way, if being positive is not in your personality, that's something that will have to change. You don't have to be the bubbly, enthusiastic kind of positive I am. But no one wants to work with a Negative Nellie. Nobody wants to entrust their home to someone who is constantly doom and gloom.

You might not have a lot of energy like I do. Maybe you're more stoic, analytical, and incredibly smart. That's a strength. Focus on it.

An agent I know is always in the Top 5 in our area. He is an extremely powerful agent and excellent at what he does. He comes across like an attorney. He's brilliant, analytical, and very calm. He isn't exciting or expressive. But he's an expert at business and finance. He attracts that type of client and, of course, they work really well together. He's completely different than I am, yet he's still very successful and does an excellent job. I respect him completely and so does the community.

When thinking about your target market, do your best to think about the kind of person that you like. Remember that even as you express who you are, you need to be unique and different in your approach, and likable. There are certainly other agents in my area who have lots of energy and enthusiasm. I still need to stand out from that crowd. **I distinguish myself by going the extra mile and being more knowledgeable than many agents with the same personality type.**

Your brand is also about your value: a) the value you give and b) the core values you hold. One of my core values is giving back, and every part of who I am expresses that. I mentioned some of my charitable work in the last chapter. I also feel a responsibility to give back in terms of helping train others in our industry, to help them become more professional and more successful. Another of my core values is in my morning affirmations: "I want to positively affect every life that I touch. I want to make sure that my clients feel special, that they know I'm listening to them, and I make time for them." Think about values that are most important to you.

As a Community Market Leader, the value you give is what you do differently. You're an entrepreneur, you treat your business like a business, and you treat your clients with the respect they deserve. You put your *all* into everything you do, you give them your best, and you are a pro. That is the value you give. My team and I have a rule in our office that we always want to be better, and we want to strive for excellence. That's what we do. It shows in our brand, not just as an empty promise, but in everything we do and say. When I created Homes By Krista, I made sure that I always gave my utmost. I always went above and beyond. Guess what? Word traveled fast. And guess what else? Clients could see that before they met me because in every single thing that I produce, I give value. When I tell clients I won't discount my commission, they have no problem with that. People are happy to pay for real value.

What value do you bring to the table? What qualities represent you, your business, your business model, and what you produce for your clients? What benefits do you give your clients that is different from your competitors?

As you become a Community Market Leader and start to dominate your market, part of your brand will be just that: You're a community leader who dominates his or her market. You're going to be seen and known everywhere. So, part of your brand will be, "Wow, I see that person everywhere." Make sure that your brand is really clear and really *you* before it starts showing up as you everywhere.

Now that my brand is everywhere, I'm attracting people who are wealthier and who have higher priced homes to sell. They are attracted by the quality, difference, and innovation of what I produce, that what I provide is different and innovative. They've seen how knowledgeable I am through my videos. They've even been attracted to the way I dress, in suits which attract a more mature and professional client.

When you're thinking about your brand, start with how you want your community to react to you, how you want them to receive you, how you want them to relate to you, and how you want to build trust with them. Really think about your strengths, personality, and the value you bring. Once you are clear about all those things, only then is it time to look into logos, business cards, the colors on your website, the photo on your signs, etc. Don't make the mistake of trying to create these pieces first before really knowing your brand.

If you are brand new in the business, you still need to develop your brand. It's not set in stone and it probably will change. Even so, you want to start standing out from the pack. What I don't recommend is that you try to promote yourself as having more experience or knowledge than you actually have. I've seen new agents do this, where they pump up their experience by showing the experience of their firm or broker. We all know that your broker is not 100% involved in the transaction, so it's dishonest to use that person's track record. And being dishonest will come back to bite you.

Instead of presenting yourself as highly experienced and knowledgeable, you can say something like this: "I am a newer agent. But let me tell you what makes me different than any other agent: I am innovative and I'm doing things differently than the people who have been in the business for fifteen to twenty years. I'm using technology and have the statistics and data to show that my approach is really effective." You can give them the example of open houses and how useless they are in the process of selling homes. "Holding an open house only helps your agent meet your neighbors and prospect for new clients who are barely entering the market and who are most likely not even qualified to purchase your home. But what I'm going to do, Mr. Seller, is use all these technologies, all these innovations, and all these techniques to expose your house to thousands more people. I have the backing of my broker who's going to walk me through every single step of the transaction. And if you have questions I can't answer, I'll tell you I don't know. I won't try to fake it. I'll find out the correct answers from my broker."

If you were approached in that way, wouldn't you respect it and be attracted by it? That's exactly what I said when I first started. Dale Carnegie wrote a classic book called *How to Win Friends and Influence People*. In it, he points out that people like to do business with people that they like. And prospective clients are going to like you if they can see that you're ethical, dedicated, determined, and that you sincerely have their best interests at heart. In California, the average seller interviews just two agents before signing a listing agreement, sometimes not even that many. If you get a foot in the door, don't waste it. Be likable, be honest, and have integrity. Give them as much value and knowledge in that listing appointment as possible. Tell them you will always make sure they're covered by staying on top of things and involving your broker. This is all part of your new brand.

Innovation

We've talked about this, but I'm going to say it again because it's critical: Once you have the vision of what kind of business you're creating and have a clear idea of your brand, you need to start incorporating innovation in all you do. If you don't, no matter how competent you are, you'll get left behind.

When I first started, one agent in our community completely ruled the market. It was unimaginable that anyone would ever be able to hold as much market share as this powerhouse agent. Today, that powerhouse is still in the ranking, but I've surpassed that person by far. Very early on, within the first year of being in business, I was neck in neck with this fierce competitor. Why? Because that person continued to do things very traditionally and did not move full speed ahead. Doing the same old thing eventually will catch up to you just as it did to that agent. Don't be like everyone else who uses the same old marketing approach that was used two, five, ten, fifteen, or twenty years ago. Do things differently, be a leader, set the new norm, and stand out from the crowd.

The very cool thing is that as soon as your competitors take notice of just how different you've become and how you've set the "new norm," you'll already be holding market share and your business will have a momentum that is unstoppable. That is where I am right now. It's insane just how busy we are and how much busier we continue to get. We don't have down time or peaks and valleys in the business, just a constant huge stream.

Initially, like everyone else, I thought there was no way I could surpass that agent. Yet, I knew if I could do things differently, and show people I am a cut above other agents by my work ethic and knowledge, eventually the community would take notice. I was clear that I had to be innovative to make them take notice. I figured that if I did that consistently for long enough, it would happen. And it happened. And guess what? It's still happening!

That previous powerhouse agent who used to be the top gun in our area—and now isn't—isn't a very common story. But it should be and it can be in your area too. My point is that most agents across the nation are not innovative. They do things the way they did them years and years ago. Don't misunderstand me - some agents have chosen a traditional real estate business model that includes making cold calls, going after expireds, and for sale by owner. It's not that this is bad. If it gets you to where you want to be, go for it! Personally, I haven't done any of that in ten years. I've never called an expired or for sale by owner, ever. In the past ten years, I've done exactly one open house only because the seller begged me. But I regretted doing it. I obtained zero results from it. Even if you see a powerhouse in your area who seems unbeatable, guess what? They are not. If you make a stand and commit to being different, to being innovative, to standing out and running your business like a business, you will be unstoppable.

My goal is to make sure that you understand how to be innovative and stay at the top of your marketplace. It's like cell phones. When they first came out forty years ago, they weighed 2½ pounds, died after 20 minutes of use, and cost about $3,000. Twenty years later, cell phones could be used as pagers, fax machines, and PDAs (personal digital assistants) to store phone numbers and keep track of your calendar. Today, you can use a cell phone to pay for Starbucks, navigate your way across town, find out the latest baseball scores, and book a trip across the world. (In 2013, the UN reported there were more people on earth with mobile phones (six billion for world population of seven billion) than there are with access to clean toilets (only 4.5 billion).)

If the cell phone industry can change that much, don't you think the real estate business should evolve as well? Look at what's happened to travel agents. They are practically extinct now because technology has taken over. If we in real estate don't change the ways they're doing things, the average real estate agent will be wiped out by innovation and technology. Those of us who choose to be different, innovative, and beyond wonderful will not only survive but thrive. You can't afford to be "just good." You have to be excellent, superb, and above great. You need to outshine everyone with your creativity, innovation drive and customer service driven work ethic!

Steve Jobs said, "Innovation distinguishes between a leader and a follower." The definition of innovation from BusinessDictionary. com is, *"The process of translating an idea or invention into a good or service, that creates value, or for which consumers will pay. To be called an **innovation**, an idea must be replicable at an economical cost and must satisfy a specific need."*

Basically, innovation is to find out some new idea, device, or method. It's the application of better solutions that meet new requirements and articulated needs, or existing market needs.

A big part of being innovative is adopting technologies that can make your business more efficient. It's about understanding how people today are finding homes and using that information—and technology— to design where and how you market yourself and your clients' properties. It's about using every new app available to you, implementing them in your business, and updating them on a regular basis.

For example, you can find reports and statistics about how buyers shop for homes: how they do their searches, what devices they use for their searches, what buyers find valuable when searching for a home, and what tools they found valuable on a website. I can go on for hours about what buyers and sellers want.

Below are a few stats from the NAR's Home Buyer and Sellers 2016 Generational Trends Report regarding the sources buyers used in looking for a home: Real Estate Agents: 89%, Websites: 89%, Websites using a Mobile Tablet: 57%, and Online Video Sites: 29%. And guess how many buyers found their new home by a yard sign or open house? Only 9%! So, if you're still relying on those to market your listings, you're out of luck.

I use these statistics to show my clients why I market the way I do and who I'm targeting. If I'm on a listing appointment, I'll show the data about how many buyers use their mobile devices for their home search. Then I show them how I use the mobile phone to forward property specific websites, show city demographics, school scores, and more to prospective buyers. I then show them what a potential buyer sees with our mobile app, how I am notified and given the buyers direct cell phone number so I can make contact. (You can reverse this to show buyers how you use apps, websites, and technology on their behalf as well.)

That said, innovation isn't just about technology. Sometimes you can come up with an idea that is better than the technology available to you. For example, I ran into a certain software at the National Association of REALTORS'® conference. It is software that you upload on an iPad. Potential buyers enter the house and pick up an iPad. They click on the iPad as they walk into each room and it tells them about the features. It is a good app, but time consuming and not very user-friendly. I tried it for a while then quit using it.

But it gave me an idea. I found someone to make very specific videos, and hone in on the home's upgrades. I have that video in the home, but also use it on the home's website and on social media so many more people are exposed to it. I use a professional videographer, so the quality is excellent. (You can find videographers on Craigslist, droners.com, tourfactory.com, or even use college students who are training in photography and videography.) The video tour takes me half the time to produce and gets blasted out for the whole internet world to see.

I don't just use pictures and string them together. I am very specific about my videos and I make sure they are unique and more interesting than others. Now I run into people on a daily basis who tell me how much they love my videos. As Agents, I think we take for granted and don't really appreciate how much people love real estate. They love to hear about it, talk about it, and give and get opinions about it. Use that to your advantage.

Which brings me to another point about innovation: Not every technology you use or idea you have will be successful. There isn't a thing I haven't tried. I've tried it all and I've failed plenty of times before I succeeded. I often figured out what *could* work by doing something that *didn't*. If you aren't failing with some of your ideas, you probably aren't stretching far enough out of the box.

I started a homeowner's support program after the real estate market tanked. I thought I could help people in distress and that it would help me financially make it through the real estate downturn. I put a lot of time and money into creating the program, but it didn't pan out in the way I'd hoped. However, I did help some people. I didn't get a lot of business from that strategy, but I had the satisfaction of helping people work through their real estate challenges. Through the program, I was able to help people save their homes and find alternatives to short sale or foreclosure. But once I took into account all of my costs, personnel and time, I really didn't make any money on it.

Since the program didn't pay off as I wanted, I made a video. I don't get contacted by many people who are having these real estate difficulties nowadays. But that video is still online and will be seen forever! That one strategy didn't work out as I'd planned, but others did. **Do not give up!** Keep trying and manipulating what you are doing.

Many years ago when I was still doing open houses, I wanted to be different. I thought, "Okay, I'm going to do an open house on a Friday night. I'll serve wine and cheese and try to attract the people coming home from work." Four people showed up. Two of them were my mom and dad and the others were neighbors. I was stuck with several bottles of wine left over. I was trying to be different, but that idea wasn't the right way to be different.

However, it did make me think about how to be different and effective. Today, when I list a house, I create a beautiful four-page colored brochure, and I have someone deliver one hundred brochures to the neighbors. The brochure says, "Please help me pick your neighbor! Deliver this to any friends or family who may be thinking about buying a home." I have the text feature printed on the flyer that brings them to the property website which has all the details about the house.

That's not only different and much more effective. This shows my seller that I am marketing to their neighbors in non-traditional way and it also shows the neighbors that I go above and beyond. They get to see my beautiful brochure, professional photography, and how I pay close attention to detail with my property descriptions. They are also exposed to the technology component on the flyer which draws them to the website/text feature. Right now, I am the only agent I know who is doing this.

It's okay to fail. It's okay to try something that's not going to work. I've been doing this for sixteen years, and failed five times to succeed once. But if you're focused on innovation, that one success will be totally outweigh all the failures.

Develop Your Niche

Have you heard the phrase, "Niches make riches?" It's true. Just about anyone can sell real estate. If you put yourself out there as a generalist, you've got a ton of competition. And you'll have to spread your marketing efforts and budget really thin to capture all categories of homes and clients. You might think that by creating a niche, you will be losing too many opportunities. You won't. By doing a good job in your niche, you will end up capturing business that is outside of it. On the other hand, if you try to relate to everybody, you won't capture anybody.

My editor always reminds me that if I try to write a book for *everybody*, it won't be very useful. The raw beginners won't understand it, it will be too simple for very experienced readers, and real estate hobbyists will think it's too much effort. By honing my message down to a specific type of reader—someone who wants to get the most out of their real estate business—I can give really clear information.

Creating a niche is also going to save you thousands of dollars in marketing. You're not throwing away marketing dollars trying to attract everyone. Instead, you focus your efforts and money on attracting the client that you want to work with. If your focus is millennials, you won't waste money on an ad in AARP, posters in the senior housing community or the men's club. You focus on text messaging, social media, and apps like Twitter, Instagram, Pinterest, and Snapchat. If you're focused on selling homes of older retirees, you won't rely solely on text blasts or mobile phone compatible landing pages or social media sites. You'll use snail mail and email, even hand deliver flyers to seniors' communities or advertise in their monthly newsletter. When you narrow in on who your client avatar is, you know exactly who to market to, how to market, whether it's on blogging, social media, any of your landing pages, your lead pages— whatever you're doing, you know who you're focusing on.

Have you ever watched an ad on TV and had absolutely no idea what the ad was about? That's because you are not that ad's target market and the advertiser doesn't care if you get it. They've designed that ad to hit home with the specific market who does understand it.

Remember, you don't have to make an impact on the entire world, you just have to reach a few. Let's put this into perspective. If you reached ten clients last year, and your goal is thirty this year, that's only twenty more people or families that you need to reach. It's not a million. If your goal is to do fifty units more, that's fifty clients you need to attract. Who do you want those fifty clients to be?

When I built my client avatar for my training and coaching program and this book, I went after a specific type of person. I went after people who are driven, competitive, and who love to learn. I targeted agents who want to be at the top of their game. Does it sound like you? That's why you were attracted to this book.

If you're having trouble finding your avatar, go back to your past clients—the good ones not the ones you wish you'd never met—and ask them, "Why did you choose me? What qualities did you like about me?" Ask them what they would have liked to have you improve in your work and relationship with them. Let them know you are open to constructive criticism. Don't be afraid to do this. You'll learn something new about yourself and your ideal client. You may also find a way to keep from losing money or how to make more money. If you hear a complaint from one person who has the courage to speak out, you probably have other clients who were unhappy. The White House Office of Consumer Affairs claims that for every customer who bothers to complain, 26 other customers remain silent.

While you're doing this, think about your good clients and what attributes they share in common. Maybe they are all smart or really diligent in doing whatever they needed to do. Maybe they are active in the community or have tight-knit families. I tend to attract great clients. Last year, out of 144, only two were horrible. I've learned how to spot red flags during a listing presentation of clients I don't want to work with. For example, I learned that if somebody is trying to beat me up over my commission, or if they've been fired multiple times, most likely they're not going to be the right client for me. It means they don't appreciate value and they're probably difficult to work with. I don't want to work with that type of person.

What are your past clients' interests? What are their desires? What do they want? If you aren't sure, ask them. What are they looking for in life? What makes them tick? Develop your client avatar with this information in mind.

In the branding section, we talked about starting with who you are and who you want your target market to be. Are you interested in first-time home buyers or sellers? Military families or vets? Would you fit best with professionals? Older couples or millennials? (By the way, the statistics on the number of millennials entering the market is staggering. If you aren't familiar with how millennials approach buying and selling, and what platforms they use, you are doing yourself and your clients a disservice.) Agents should be flexible enough to work with just about anyone, but who would you love to work with? What group of people would you like to cultivate as clients? If you work with people who are at odds with you, the transaction is going to be much more difficult. Personally, I don't want to fight my clients in a tug of war over dominance. I want my clients to trust me and know that I have their best interests at heart. Learn to say "no" to clients that aren't a fit so you can focus on the clients you want. In the Resources section at the end of this book, you'll find an example Client Avatar Worksheet. Use that worksheet to create the perfect client avatar for yourself.

Next, figure out what type of real estate you want to work with. Low end homes or higher end homes? Older neighborhoods or new developments? Do you want to specialize in a certain neighborhood or zip code? Fixer-uppers? Investment properties? Condos? Properties by the water or beach? Ranch properties?

Personally, I decided to focus on high-end homes. Why? Because I'm educated with a Masters' degree. I value learning and respect others who have pursued education. I also relate to people who are experts in their field and have done well in what they do. I felt that this is the type of client who would appreciate those aspects of me. And going after this type of client has helped my average sales price be 2.6% higher than the average sales price in one of the main cities in which I focus.

I also decided to focus just on sellers. At a certain point, I decided that buyers are too much work. I was out showing property constantly. I was writing offers and presenting them on weekends and evenings. I had to do everything based on my clients' availability. I'd had enough of that, so I shifted my focus.

My niche became selling high end homes in the Brentwood and Oakley areas of Northern California. The homes I focus on range from $550K to $750K. Does it sound too narrow? Keep in mind that I'm able to do 12 to 14 transactions every month in this niche and that number is increasing not decreasing.

People who can afford to own high end homes often have a combination of professionalism and education. I started marketing to those people. I didn't just target them. I marketed in the language they speak and distributed through the avenues they are most comfortable using. I created events and shared information they would find interesting and valuable. I literally changed the way I dress to attract that type of client!

Changing how you dress may sound extreme but think about it. If you were an attorney, would you have a better first impression of someone in a sharp suit or someone wearing cargo pants and a sweater? If you were a rancher, would you feel more comfortable with someone who showed up in jeans or someone dressed in haute couture? It's back to the brand: When you decide the kind of business you want, *everything* should reflect that niche.

In the very beginning, I used to dress more provocatively. I was single and young, and I didn't even realize the impression I was making. Then I started to realize people weren't taking me seriously as a business person. By my appearance, no one would assume that I could handle big ticket transactions. I knew I needed to change—but how? It's funny that my parents had complained about my attire for years and I didn't listen. Once I saw that how I dressed was negatively impacting my business, I immediately made different fashion choices. (My parents got a real kick out of reading this!)

This is where emulating someone who is successful comes in. I went online and researched agents throughout the country who were working with higher-end homes, who had a lot of education. I studied how they presented themselves in every aspect of their lives. Not just their dress, but how they marketed, what their team was like, what they were doing differently. I took the best of what I found and figured out how to improve on it. I watched T.V. shows like *Scandal* (I love Olivia Pope's style!), with high-powered attorneys and businesswomen. And there you have it: Krista's new style was born.

You may not yet know your niche. Let me give you some examples to inspire your thinking. I heard of an agent in the La Jolla area. She specialized in clients from Mexico who wanted to purchase vacation homes in the U.S. She had lived in Mexico for a while herself, spoke Spanish, and knew the culture. She also had personal connections with several wealthy people from that country. She built her business completely by referral, initially using her connections. She gave personalized service (picking clients up at the airport, booking their hotel rooms, showing them around the city, etc.), translated escrow documents, and was experienced in foreign exchange rates. Her business grew with hardly any marketing effort on her part.

Another example: In my area, most of the community is residential homes but about 10% of the real estate is farms and land. One agent I know targets people who own farms and live on acres of rural/agricultural land. Even though that's a small percentage of the population, she is one of the top five agents in the area because she's focusing, specializing, and meeting the direct needs of a specific type of person and property. She knows all about septic tanks, wells, and easements specific to agricultural property. She knows all the different rules for square footage in out-buildings, whether you can have animals and what type of animals you can have. If you're selling or buying that kind of property, you'd absolutely go to her because regular agents simply don't have the knowledge and experience she's acquired over the years. She makes sure people know that she's an expert in this niche. Whenever I have a land deal or custom home on acreage, I call her to make sure I'm not missing anything.

Think about this. If you speak Spanish fluently, wouldn't it be a great market to target? If I did, I would hook up with a Spanish speaking lender and market that like nobody's business. I suggested this to a fellow Realtor in my area and he hasn't heeded my advice. I wish he would as I know it would be prosperous for him. Your niche can help define you and attract clients because you specialize in exactly what they are looking for. If you just sound like everyone else, they'd probably overlook you. It doesn't mean that you won't get clients outside your niche. Some agents worry that if they specialize too much or have too specific a niche, it will harm them. I totally disagree on that notion.

How about if you live in an area with a lot of condos? I know of an agent who rules the high-rise condo market in San Diego. He calls himself The Condo King, and he's killing it. If you're selling a condo, you're selling it through him. He knows what each condo development allows or doesn't allow, how many dogs you can have, or if you can't have any dogs at all. He knows what the association fees are, and if your condo has to be owner-occupied or if it can be a rental. Thinking as a consumer, isn't he the guy you'd go to if you wanted a condo in San Diego? Through his marketing, he tells you that he knows *everything* you need to know about condos in that area.

What is your niche? Be as specific as you possibly can. Be neighborhood specific, not city specific. Think of a specific type of home and specific kind of client. I know it seems counter intuitive. But with a smaller, tighter net, you'll catch a lot more fish! Start out small and as you begin to dominate that niche, then you can expand. Start by being super laser-focused, committed, and consistent about your marketing efforts into that specific niche. At first, I worked to become really well known in two specific neighborhoods, Deer Ridge and Shadow Lakes. Very quickly, after having success in those two neighborhoods, I expanded into my entire town, Brentwood. But I didn't add to my farm until I had completely dominated each area, saturated it consistently, and made myself known— what I call Location Domination. Then I replicated this into another area, and so on and so on.

Stay Ahead of the Trends

What I'm going to say next may sound contradictory to the last section. Bear with me.

Creating your niche is critical to your success. But don't be swimming upstream in the market. Get *ahead* of the market by knowing what's coming down the pike.

What do I mean by that? Let me tell you my own story.

Even in the beginning of my career, I always researched market trends. I tried to anticipate, based upon data and analytics, how the real estate market would be affected in the future. In the years 2005-2007, we had a fantastic seller's market. Suddenly, I realized that home prices were increasing too fast. Common sense told me that something was going to happen. It is impossible for a house—in one month, on the same street, and a model match—to go from $400,000 to $475,000. But, that is what was happening. I figured something had to break.

I started researching banks. I figured out people would soon start losing their homes. I knew we were going to have a problem. I started contacting banks, traveling the country, and going to bankers' association conferences. By the time the real estate market completely crashed in 2008, I had already started going to banking foreclosure conferences and establishing relationships with banks and asset managers. By being pro-active, thinking ahead, educating myself, and doing my research, I landed over thirteen banks and asset management companies, and helped them sell their foreclosures. Looking back, I would never want to do that kind of business again. It was sad and depressing, but at the time, it was survival. Many agents lost their homes, careers, and disappeared—until the market got easy again a few years ago.

By the time the market totally crashed, I was already working with thirteen different banks selling their foreclosures. By then, it was almost too late for anyone else to get in, make the connections, and have the expertise they needed to sell foreclosures. From 2008 to 2014, my focus was foreclosures and short sales.

I kept my finger on the pulse of the market. By 2014, values were getting closer to where values had been previously. I could see the foreclosures lessening and asset management companies selling off their portfolios to larger banks. It seemed likely that we'd have a more traditional market within six to twelve months. People were going to have more equity in their homes. So, it was time for me to reposition myself from a foreclosure and short sale specialist, to an area specialist in high end properties.

I headed to a course called the Institute for Luxury Home Marketing. I started to brand myself and my properties as if each listing I took—whether it was a $400,000 or a $700,000 listing—was a million-dollar listing. I mass marketed everywhere, social media, mailers, online, Google. All of my materials looked like million-dollar listings. People started noticing. "This person, she's doing something different. She's sending out full color four-page brochures. She's creating full blown virtual property tours, and social media ads."

None of this happened by accident. I paid attention and educated myself on what factors affect the market. I used common sense to anticipate what was going to happen. Then I positioned myself to respond to what was happening before most agents in the market even realized it was changing.

I know some agents in my area who were lucky and fell into the foreclosure market using the connections of relatives and friends. They also did well during that period. However, they didn't anticipate the market and get the real expertise they needed. Then they didn't anticipate the return of a more traditional market, so they didn't reposition themselves and go for the expertise they'd need in a new market. Most of them are gone entirely or doing less than half the business I'm doing. **The difference is anticipation and preparation.**

In the business world, we have a famous example of a business giant that did *not* anticipate and prepare: IBM. IBM actually started in the 1880's and grew to be the leader in the new industry of computers. It became a huge organization with a conservative business model that couldn't (or didn't) shift directions swiftly enough. IBM researchers actually developed many of the technologies we see today. However, they did not anticipate how these technologies would completely change the landscape of their industry.

In the 1990's, the popularity of PC's and client servers completely undermined IBM's core mainframe business. It was called "the PC revolution" as millions of people bought computers for personal and small business use. Next came "the client/server revolution" which allowed all of those personal computers to become linked. Though IBM had access to that technology, it didn't see what was coming and didn't capitalize on it. IBM almost went under, and it took a painful reorganization for the company to survive.

As you create your business, stay flexible. Educate yourself about the market: What's happening? How is the absorption rate trending? What's going on in the community, locally? What's happening nationally? How does that affect the seller? How does that affect the buyer? How does that affect what's happening now and what could possibly happen later?

And how can your business remain responsive to all of that?

Use Technology for Efficiency and Impact

I could not do all I do without automating a lot of my processes. Let me tell you about a couple of technologies that are really helpful. For example, I use Realvolve for my client relationship management (CRM) platform. You can research other CRM's out there and figure out which is best for you. Personally, I use Realvolve because it is so easy to use, has all the features I love, and is cost-effective.

I have a number of people working with me and each one has certain tasks to do. We have specific protocols for everything we do, and we've loaded Realvolve with our processes so it can track our activity and generate checklists to keep us on point. Everything is task-driven and we're very systematic about what specific activities happen during each phase of every marketing campaign, listing appointment, or transaction.

For example, in a transaction we have the marketing phase, the escrow phase, and the closing phase. Once we plug in the start dates of an individual phase, Realvolve uses that date to create start dates and deadlines for each activity based on the standard process we've created for that phase. Whether it is calls to be made or forms to be completed, Realvolve tracks the tasks and who is assigned to each task. Transaction checklists are generated with deadlines. Reminders go out via text message and email to the team, and even to the client, a few days before each task deadline. When a task is completed, Realvolve records it. The paperwork of each transaction is also stored with Realvolve for easy access.

Let me run you through one of our lead generation processes to show you how we work.

It starts when we set up a social media campaign using Facebook ads. I create a few videos that lead potential sellers to a landing page that has home valuation software. When someone goes to that page and fills out the form to receive an automatic valuation, we capture their information and it goes directly to Realvolve. Buyer inquiries from Zillow or my website also go directly into Realvolve. All of these are now valid buyer and seller leads.

Realvolve allows us to "tag" each contact in a way that will immediately set up that lead as an active buyer or seller. Then a campaign is set up for that person, so we can set it and forget it. We also have texting features. If a potential buyer enquires about a specific property, the text message gives them the URL for the property's website. It also captures their contact information so I or someone from my office can quickly follow up with a call. We also email a property brochure and a Home Buyer's Guide to them. They are offered the chance to opt-in to my buyers' campaign and informational video emails. Within a few minutes of contacting us, a potential buyer is given valuable information automatically.

If it is a seller lead, the same sort of process happens. We send seller's tips, videos, and brochures to make sure we give them as much value as possible. When we receive an inquiry from a seller, or someone requests a valuation, or if we are contacted through my website, Zillow, or any other site, Realvolve sends his or her contact information directly to me so I can follow up immediately with a call. (We all know that the first to respond is usually the one who gets the listing.) A person in my office is notified to hand deliver a CMA (current market analysis) to that potential seller and we also email the CMA. Then my staff is reminded via Realvolve to send a card two days after the first inquiry saying, "Hey thank you for your interest. Be sure to check your e-mail for some valuable information. We also dropped it off on your porch." We then follow this with a video e-mail.

These campaigns are "set it and forget it" programs with information the buyer or seller can really use. They're customized by Realvolve so they're excellent and look great. They're not like the standard campaign most agents use. Our campaigns focus on the needs of the buyer or seller, not on "Wow, look at how great I am!"

Once the buyer or seller sets up an appointment, Realvolve creates a schedule of all the tasks for the next phase. When a buyer lead sets up an appointment, Realvolve sends them a copy of the Buyer's Guide if they haven't yet received one. Our buyers' agents are given the specs of what kind of home the buyer is interested in so they can start sending information on homes that match their interest. Our agents call the buyer and put them in touch with one of our lenders so they can be pre-qualified. We send out our video on Do's and Don'ts for buyers. We give them in-depth information about the area from nearby amenities to tax rates. We also explain to them how we work differently than other buyers' agents.

When a seller makes an appointment, my assistant drops off my brochure that talks about all I do and what makes me different. Just dropping off that brochure before the appointment makes me look 100% better than anyone else. Consciously or unconsciously, the seller is thinking, "Wow she went out of her way to do this. She's on top of things." They can tell that is the way I run my entire business.

The day before the appointment, Realvolve also sends them a video of my listing presentation. I introduce it by saying, "Here's my listing presentation. Please look at this before our meeting because it shows you a lot about what I what I have to offer and my marketing techniques. My goal is to add as much value as I can to you. I want to be respectful of your time. This video will really prepare you so you know what questions you will want to ask me." This saves me so much time at the appointment. The seller is prepared with really good questions. And I'm not spending time selling my marketing plan because they have already seen it through the video. I also let them know that my marketing approach is constantly being updated and changed, and that every home is marketed differently based on its unique qualities. I also let them know that the actual marketing process is way more extensive than I or the video could truly show.

Before the appointment, I think of all the materials I'll need for the meeting, like tax roll, current market analysis, and neighborhood information. All of this goes into Evernote, which feeds directly into Realvolve, and is loaded onto my iPad so I can refer to it during the appointment. I also load my Listing Checklist on my iPad. With this checklist, all I have to do is check off items and make notes from questions I ask during the appointment. (For example, "Why are you moving? How much do you owe?") This information automatically goes into Google Docs under the seller's name.

The Seller's Check List also includes items such as, "Call carpet cleaners for estimate" or "Send referrals for window cleaners." It's already pre-written with little checkboxes. As soon as the information is in Evernote, my staff can see it and know what they have to do after the appointment. And again, this is automatically fed into Realvolve, which also reminds us to send a "thank you for meeting with me" card. I put a comment in Google Docs so the card is personalized to the client directly.

Once we have the listing, we move the seller's file into the pre-marketing phase. Realvolve sends out the Seller's Homework to prepare the seller for the marketing specialist so their meeting is productive. (A copy of our Seller's Homework is in the Resources section). We then notify our stagers to make an appointment with the seller. All appointments are put in the calendar on Realvolve so it automatically will send email and text message reminders of the times and dates of appointments. We capture the date when the stager will do the actual staging so we can automatically schedule pictures, video, and marketing appointments.

In the next phase, when the house is being actively marketed, we have specific protocols about how and when various marketing materials go out. (I talk about this in detail in Chapter Three.) Each staff member has certain tasks during the marketing phase and Realvolve sends out reminders to us all.

One thing I want to point out here is that we shift our protocols to be responsive to the market. Right now we're in a seller's market, so we can set up an "offer deadline date" to encourage buyers to move quickly. Obviously, we wouldn't do this in a buyer's market. You need to stay flexible and tweak each phase to make sense with market conditions.

I talk about what happens next in the transaction phase in detail in Chapter Three. The important thing to note here is that *anything* you do can be made simpler and more efficient by good use of technology. It keeps the team or a solo agent organized, informed, and able to retrieve information quickly. Rather than you reminding everybody about deadlines, your CRM can send out texts to your client and team that say, "Contingency due in 3 days" or "Update Zillow ad." Any reminders for appointments, anything and everything, go through Realvolve. Because everything is run through our CRM, if someone gets sick or is on vacation, someone else can step in and know exactly what's been done and what they need to do next. The technology helps us make sure that nothing drops through the cracks.

I also save time by using a company called Core Fact. By using Core Fact, all of my marketing materials are set up in templates. I have five or six different templates of my brochure. The templates are branded and professional, so all my team has to do is go in and tweak information. I don't have to recreate a new piece every time. For example, I have "Just Sold" templates, one for sending electronically and one for snail mail postcards. When we're ready to send one out, my team just goes into Core Fact and fills in information about the houses that were sold. Then, they're automatically sent out to my various lists. I didn't always do it that way, but now that I'm busier it's worth it to me to spend money on this technology. I can spend a little bit more money to make a lot more.

Realvolve retains all information about prospective buyers and sellers, as well as current and past clients. It keeps track of our interactions with them and personal information like birthdays, anniversaries, and the anniversary of their sale or purchase so we can send out cards. We also drop off a CMA every six months letting them know their house value (by the way, people *love* this). Whenever I pull up a file, I have all the information on that person and our dealings at my fingertips.

By the way, here's how I do standard videos to be efficient: I make a really good, upbeat generic happy birthday video. Then when our CRM sends it out, the email subject line itself says, "Hi, John Doe. I just wanted to make sure I caught you on your special day." They click on the video and it's like a continuation of the greeting. So, even though it's generic, it feels personal.

One issue I'm having right now is that my business is booming (great problem to have, right?). We're on track to do about 150 transactions this year which means I have zero time to make personal phone calls to keep in touch with past clients. The videos allow me to keep connected and to show that I care about them and what is happening in their lives. They tell me that they see me so often in my videos that they hardly notice that I haven't called!

Realvolve interfaces with another technology I use, BombBomb. BombBomb sends out all of my video emails and tracks their open rates. It also has a feature that auto-detects the recipient's devices and connection speeds, then it sends the optimal video format to them. Once you set it up, it's another "set it and forget it" type of thing. The best thing is that BombBomb now has an advanced option to ensure you don't miss anything. It's super easy and mobile phone compatible which makes it convenient and ensures you'll use it.

You need to be tracking the traffic and effectiveness of your posts and emails. For example, if you send 100 emails, how many are really getting the word out? Say, ten of them bounce for bad addresses. Ninety get delivered and ten of those are opened. Then how many of those people take the next step? Your CRM should be able to tell you so you can tweak what you're doing to get better open and conversion rates. Our CRM is very specific and can tell us the exact demographics—gender, age range, location—of who is opening and clicking through. This helps us focus on the correct target market for a particular property.

One note about email: Be careful about becoming identified as a spammer. If you blast out too many emails, Google takes notice. We always try to get contacts on our lists to opt in, especially to our video market updates.

You can access other reports that will tell you how effective your ads and posts are. For example, we're on a program with Zillow where we can go in and optimize our listings on the site (Zillow has all sorts of classes and programs so you can get the most out of using it). We then get analytics from Zillow that tells us how much more effective our ads are than others in terms of numbers of opens and click throughs. We can use this to show our sellers, "Hey, your ad got 87% more traffic than any other homes similar to yours."

With the analytics, we can tell if we need to change something to get more traffic, maybe by using a different photo or tweaking the wording. We can also see when a home is getting a lot of online traffic, but is sitting on the market too long with few showings. This typically means it's priced too high. When we show our clients this data, they are more comfortable agreeing to a price reduction.

Another software we use is Agent Marketing. With Agent Marketing, you input all the information on a specific home and it automatically kicks out a Craigslist ad, an e-flyer, or any piece you set up. You can also input an address and it will produce a wealth of area data like school scores, location of golf courses and parks, restaurants, shopping—just about anything a buyer would want to know. We use all of this in our marketing pieces. And, we show this to our sellers so they know what we are doing on their behalf.

For the contracts and documents of a transaction, we use Realvolve and combine Docusign which allows us to do digital signatures. The software puts everything on a CD at the end of the transaction so the file is all in one easy-to-access place.

Again, the point is to train yourself to think, "What technology is available to make each process better, smoother, more innovative and easier? What will help save you time and make you more money?"

Get Support You Need

Even with the efficiencies of technology, as you start grasping what it really means to be Community Market Leader, you'll probably think, "Yikes! That's a lot of work!" It is. And as you progress, though you can do a lot of it yourself, you are going to have to get some help and put some money into it.

Please remember, this is *your* business. You cannot expect to make a decent living without spending money to make money. All successful businesses have expenses. They allocate money for marketing, employee costs, and equipment. Any other business typically has a lot more expenses than you'll ever incur. The investment you make into your business will pay off, guaranteed. Keep in mind that you don't have to build up your support system all at once. Take it in steps.

In the beginning, I did everything alone. In that first year in the business when I sold 69 homes, mainly all buyers, I did every single thing by myself. If you recall, my first year was the year my world was turned upside down. I had no money, an empty bank account, two children, yet I was still able to put 69 buyers into homes just by being different in what I did.

I had to think outside of the box to stand out without spending a bunch of money I didn't have. I did things in baby steps. When everyone else was making one-page black and white flyers for their listings, I spent a few precious dollars to create four-page color brochures. When I went on tours with buyers, I made colored print outs with comment sections in the order of the homes we were going to see. Yes, it was a tad more costly than what others were doing. But it definitely helped me close those 69 homes. Just that one difference in the way I did things made people sit up and take notice.

So, keep being innovative and unique, even on a shoestring budget. Then as you start to make money, it's time to set up a real marketing budget. I recommend a 20% marketing budget. This may sound steep but it will make so much more money for you as you move forward. Again, you have to be thinking like an entrepreneur. One article I read recently stated:

- Companies that grew 1-15% year over year spent an average of 16.5% of their revenue on marketing

- Companies that grew 16-30% year over year spent an average of 22% of their revenue on marketing

- Companies that grew 31-100+% year over year spent an average of 50.2% of their revenue on marketing[1]

I work with about 20% and it works for me. For example, the numbers just came out for 2016 as I'm writing this. In the county I dominate, I sold 144 homes. My next closest competitor, who is a super top-producing agent in East County, sold 60. The next highest ranking producers were way below that.

[1] http://www.sbmarketingtools.com/much-spend-marketing/

To do that much business, you need support. The key is to figure out your own "highest and best use." In other words, sure, you can do it all (and burn yourself out). But the questions you should be asking are: What am I doing that no one else can do as well? What am I doing that someone with much less knowledge and training can do? What am I doing that is not my strength and not fun for me? Those are the things you want someone else to handle.

In my third year, as I made more money and improved, I hired an assistant who worked twenty hours per week to make the CDs of the video home tours I did at that time and to handle the colored brochures. (This was fourteen years ago, CDs and colored brochures were very forward thinking back then!) Rather than spending time making CDs and colored flyers, I focused on improving myself, researching new technologies that could help my business, and coming up with unique, innovative ideas. And, of course, I still handled all the face time with my clients.

If I could only give you three pieces of advice, here's what they would be: 1) Do video, no matter what kind of video it is (though an educational piece is best). 2) Hire an assistant. Even if you need to take out a loan or eat Top Ramen for a month, hire an assistant. This will enable you to do things that you can't do on your own. You'll be able to research the latest technologies or take a class on innovative strategy, then have your assistant implement what you've learned. The more new and innovative techniques and practices you implement, the more you'll reap the benefits in new clients and closings. People do take notice. 3) Hire a coach. This is your business and if you want to succeed and truly turn your business into a steam engine that never stops, hire someone to help guide and push you through it.

Recently, I went on three listing presentations in two days and I won all three. Two were at full commission. The third was an $800,000 listing, which is high in my area. I came in at the highest commission. The seller really wanted me and asked if I would handle the sale for ½% less. They were a referral, so I obliged and felt good about it. My point is that it is getting easier and easier for me to close deals because my clients see all that I do for them. My work stands out. I'm so incredibly busy because of the value that I give—and I couldn't give all that value without support.

Please don't think that by reading this book, taking webinars, or attending classes you'll instantly succeed and see dramatic changes in your business. To see change, you need to implement the practices and heed the advice you're given. If you're not willing to do that, then put this book down, run your business like the 95% of all the other agents out there, and be satisfied with the results you get.

If you're ready to find the help you need to grow, you'll find lots of leads for virtual assistants via the web. (I've listed references at the end of this chapter.) You can find sharp local college students who want to work part-time or semi-retired folks who are eager to keep active. Be very specific about the skills you need and choose someone who is tech-savvy.

When you interview them, just make sure they have the same drive for excellence that you have. Look for someone who is an independent worker so you don't spend too much of your precious time supervising them. And once you hire someone, be *very* clear about what you need them to do. Present a *detailed* job description of what you expect from them before you hire them.

Today, I have six people working for me in addition to three buyers' agents. I have a full-time professional videographer and photographer. Rather than paying someone to do 12-14 house shoots per month, it's more economical and efficient to have her on staff. I have a full-time Digital Marketer who takes care of our online digital platform, and a Marketing Specialist and an Assistant Marketing Specialist who deal with print and social media. All three help implement new strategies and continually upgrade our marketing efforts. I have a Transaction Coordinator and an Assistant Transaction Coordinator who make sure each transaction runs smoothly. I also have three agents who are buyers' specialists. They have their own book of business, but I also pay them to drive my buyers around and show them homes. Once my buyers find a home they want, I step back in and do all the negotiations, handling the transaction from contract to close.

Here's a job description for the person in my marketing position (keep in mind most of these tasks are done through Realvolve):

- ✓ Check my marketing email account and take care of any emails that need to be answered right away.
- ✓ Check Google KEEP and make sure everything is taken care of the same day
- ✓ Check Calendar for daily tasks
- ✓ Sign onto KCM and post personal article every day to all social media sites
- ✓ Check Facebook and respond to comments, messages and upload all new properties and market updates to business page (market updates to personal page also)
- ✓ Check LinkedIn, Twitter, and Instagram. Upload all property marketing to these sites
- ✓ Check supplies of paper, ink for printer, CMA/listing presentation materials, and all office supplies
- ✓ Clean the office and bathroom weekly
- ✓ Take care of any issue with the printer
- ✓ Print CMA cover sheets, magazine print out, and tear sheet
- ✓ Create multiple postcards to send to farm areas
- ✓ Create custom backs for postcards
- ✓ Request loan scenarios on all properties to add to brochure
- ✓ Order USPS slips for monthly marketing postcards

- ✓ Take inventory of what other Realtors® print
- ✓ Make sure Krista's website is up to date and has newest videos on it
- ✓ Keep count of all brochures printed and send list to lender monthly
- ✓ Give stager new contact info and email clients seller homework (input Realvolve dates)
- ✓ Check-in weekly with all new upcoming listings
- ✓ Schedule video and photo shoots with clients once stager has staged property
- ✓ Inform photographer/videographer of all upcoming homes and add them into the calendar for KM
- ✓ Request signs to be installed
- ✓ Complete description of home for detailed marketing
- ✓ Update contacts after viewing the home
- ✓ Send seller's professional photos
- ✓ Create "Coming Soon" listing on Zillow and Facebook
- ✓ Send clients "Coming Soon" marketing
- ✓ Begin my pre-marketing stage of listing the home
- ✓ Request special dates for family / Update Realvolve & Google
- ✓ Create property website on Agent Marketing and assign a text rider
- ✓ Generate and create List Reports (www.ListReports.com, free service)
- ✓ Once property website is fully created, send link to client that explains everything the website does

✓ Download property tour once done, and add to YouTube, FB, LinkedIn, Twitter, and Instagram, and also send to client

✓ Upload video to Zillow

✓ Design "Just Listed" postcard and property brochure, and send both to client

✓ Double check all online marketing is complete

✓ Make sure Realvolve has correct information on the contact and it is tagged correctly

✓ Apply correct task plans to ensure all tasks are being completed

✓ Create MLS partial listing and send to client for review

✓ Assign Supra lock box to MLS listing before installing at the home

✓ Tell Krista to call client to let them know home is on MLS

✓ Send them Sellers Beware video

✓ Deliver super, combo, and brochures to the property

✓ Send all buyers' specialists new listing info

✓ Complete MLS and make property active, and send to clients w/BombBomb video and pdf

✓ Give marketing updates every Monday and Friday (including video results on FaceBook, Zillow interest, MLS interest, Craigslist link, Realtor.com link and updated Craigslist link, Mass e-flyer, multiple postcards that feature their home, and all social media uploads

✓ Once offer is received, place "I'm taken" rider on lawn sign

✓ Double check client's photo was requested for closing gift

✓ Once received, order it on shutterfly.com and have shipped to gift center

- ✓ Complete the logo on back and wrap with card for Krista to deliver
- ✓ Add KM logo and wrap in burlap for her to deliver by final signing
- ✓ Request lawn sign to be removed
- ✓ Collect lock box and combo box
- ✓ Create "Just Sold" postcard and send to printer (using Corefact)
- ✓ Update Excel spreadsheet of all homes closed and coming up
- ✓ Update and review Realvolve daily (complete tasks as needed and add new people into contacts while tagging properly)
- ✓ Tag in Realvolve as Past Seller/Buyer and casino party if Krista requests for them to be on the list
- ✓ Request all forwarding info and special dates, if we didn't receive them prior
- ✓ If Buyer, get the date of their closing so we can send 6 month and 1 year anniversary CMAs
- ✓ Update contacts with closing date and price
- ✓ Make sure testimonials are requested
- ✓ When we receive a testimonial then add to KM website
- ✓ Add past sales to Zillow

There's no way I could be as effective as I am if I had to do all of this by myself! Figure out how you can afford hiring people and get yourself some good help so you can focus on building your business and creating new ideas, rather than staying stuck in day to day operational details.

Here are some resources I've used to help get me the support I need:

- HireMyMom.com
- Fiverr.com
- Upnest.com
- Myoutdesk.com
- Upwork.com
- Realestatevirtualassistant.com

Your assistants can help you with creating things like landing pages, lead pages, videos with graphics, brochures, creative flyers, and post cards.

Fit Your Business to Your Life

I'd like you to start with the attitude that *you* run your business, *it* doesn't run you. I know, I know—if you're just starting out, it doesn't feel that way. It feels like you have to answer every call at 10pm on Sunday night, chase every slim chance of a listing or potential buyer, and host a gazillion open houses. But even if you're a raw newbie, take a deep breath and say, "I run my business. It doesn't run me." And if you've been in our business for 16 years, stop right now and affirm, "From this point on, I run my business. It doesn't run me." Honestly, people respect you when you have boundaries. They respect you when you tell them that after 7pm you turn your phone off, and that Sundays are family days. Let's be honest, if clients don't respect your boundaries or appreciate that you'll be able to give them better service if you have a little personal time with yourself and your family, then you don't want to work with them anyway.

As a Community Market Leader, you're not just about making a living. You're creating the life you really want.

Personally, I wake up every morning between 4:30 and 5:30. I haven't always done that. I like to sleep. I love to sleep! But I've realized I get so much more energy when I wake up early. I tackle half my day before half the world is even awake (especially in real estate, because most agents get up at 9am, drink their coffee, and show up to the office around 11am). I get up in the morning, go to the gym for an hour five days a week, then come home and hit my emails. I make sure I answer questions and communicate with my clients early in the day, so they realize they're important to me.

After emails, I take some kind of educational course for an hour or so. When I take educational courses or online training, it just gives me energy. I'm learning something new and I'm excited about it. I feel alive and awake. With this routine, my day starts with energy, excitement, and enthusiasm.

In the beginning when I did everything myself, I had a similar routine to start my day, but it wasn't to this extent. I was at the beck and call of buyers and had to put in more hours at the office to get the results I wanted to get. But as you start to grow financially, and as your units start to grow, so does your business model and how you manage your time.

Now, I tell my sellers I'm not available on Sundays and I'm not available after 7pm. I tell them I am available 7am to 7pm, Monday through Friday. If it's an emergency, they can call me on Saturday. And I let them know if Realtors® call me on Saturday, I take their calls. But I don't take any calls on Sunday. I'll respond to them next business day. Nothing can happen on Sunday anyway because the banks are closed.

I learned I had to set clear boundaries with my sellers, and they respect it. The ones that don't, I don't want to work with. I have to set boundaries with other agents, as well. When they call me on the weekend or late at night, I politely remind them that if I answered every call and e-mail the moment they came in, I'd *never* get a day off. I need downtime so I can stay sharp.

Agents are so used to working weekends and nights that sometimes they take offense that I won't just jump at their whims. I've even had agents try to use it against me by calling my sellers and saying, "I couldn't get in touch with your agent"— even if they only called 25-45 minutes before. I don't want you to feel that you owe anyone an explanation. Run your business so you have the personal and family time you need. If you don't, you will burn out and be less effective for your clients. I explain this and my clients almost always understand.

The sellers and agents who respect my boundaries and my family time are the kind of people I want to work with. And I've found they respect me more for doing it. My boundaries help me sustain my energy level. I tell clients, "If I worked 24/7, I would not be giving you my best." Everyone needs a day off. Unfortunately, for some odd reason, agents don't think people in real estate do.

What are your boundaries? How do you need to set up your work schedule so you have a healthy balance?

I have two business coaches, is younger than I am. She teaches professionals how to be better at their jobs. She completely sets boundaries. When my children were younger and I made client calls from home, I used to worry about it. "If anybody hears my kids in the background, they're going to think I'm unprofessional." But this coach encourages boundaries. During training calls with her, you can hear her kids in the background, yet she's totally focused on you. She gives her family good family time, and her clients good client time. When she works from home, she's so excellent at what she does that I don't think twice about her kids being in the background. I think, "Wow, she's amazing. She's on this call, in her house, with her children, and makes a difference in her kids' lives while making a difference in ours." That's how powerful and good she is at her job. I respect how she has decided to run her business and how she has set her boundaries, because she is giving me incredible value.

On the other hand, if you work from home and treat your business like a hobby instead of a business, it's not going to fly.

Don't Sell Your Soul

Commission-based work can be tough. Most real estate agents need to sell a client's house more than the client does. It comes across in the way they do their business. These agents are focused only on closing the deal. They're so worried about closing the deal, they forget about the people involved. Real estate becomes a money thing, not a people thing. Here's where one of my slogans applies again: "People before things, always. If you do your best to take care of people, the things will always come."

I don't think most people in real estate engage in fraudulent behavior—although there is too much of that in our industry. I think many agents are susceptible to doing less than their best. For example, it's not that uncommon to see a listing that is obviously over-priced. Why? The listing agent probably knows that it's over-priced but, to land the listing, they inflated the price to impress the seller. Or, even worse, the agent didn't have the guts to tell the seller that they were way out of line for fear of losing the listing. Every seller thinks that their house is the very best house on the block and worth more than anyone else's, even though the comparable homes tell another story. Over-pricing a house will not help you or the seller.

On the rare occasions that I don't get a listing, it's typically because the seller has over-priced their home. I cannot tell you how many times I decline a listing due to a seller's unrealistic price expectation. They choose to hire an agent that tells them what they want to hear, and, when they don't get any action on the house, I end up with the listing several months later. At that point, the seller is ready to do whatever I say. A house sells when it is priced right. Don't waste their time or yours. That isn't how a Community Market Leader acts.

When I find myself in this situation, I make sure that I'm giving the client more information than anybody else has. I don't tell them they're wrong because I don't want to put them on the defensive. Instead, I say, "I'm on your team. My objective is to make sure I get you the best price possible on the best terms for you." Then, I educate them. I show them statistically that when you price a home where it should be, it is exposed to more potential buyers and they have a better opportunity to make more money.

I show clients the charts and graphs that point out how much longer it takes overpriced houses to sell, the number of price reductions that typically occur, and how most sellers end up actually selling their homes for *less* than they would have if they had priced it competitively in the first place. I show them examples of homes that were similar and priced correctly, and how much more quickly those homes ended up selling for more money because they attracted more potential buyers. You all know the drill. Don't be afraid to tell the truth and follow it up with facts. The data doesn't lie and sellers can usually see it.

It's all about being on their team, and truly having their best interest at heart. When you walk into a listing where the seller is fixated on an unrealistic price, you've got your work cut out for you. You need to show up armed with information. And, you need to be willing to walk away. I didn't get this at first, but now I am not afraid to say, "Hey, as much as I want your business and know I'm the best person for this job, I'm not going to take your listing. I don't want to waste your time or mine, and I don't want to disappoint you. I know if I take your listing at that price, I will disappoint you. I want to under-promise and over-deliver. And at that price, it's going to hurt you, not help you, and I can't do that."

Will you lose that business? Maybe. But usually you gain respect. You've shown them your value by being the expert and educating them on how over-pricing a home can shoot them in the foot. You've shown that you have integrity. If they think you'll take any listing and do anything they ask, they're going to walk all over you. More importantly, on some level, you won't feel good about yourself.

A friend of mine told me a story from when she was in her twenties. She had inherited a bunch of money and decided she wanted to buy a fixer-upper, renovate it, and then sell it. She was pretty naïve back then, but fortunately got hooked up with a very honest agent (who happened to be a single mom and fairly new to the business). My friend found a fixer that she thought was perfect. She was all set to make an offer when her agent said, "I couldn't sleep at all last night thinking about your buying this house. It would be a disaster for you." She pointed out all the problems with the house and how difficult they would be to fix. My friend ended up not making that offer.

But you know what happened? She bought another fixer through the same agent that was less of a challenge. As my friend became more experienced, she sold the first house and bought another. Then she sold that house and bought a duplex. She ended up buying and selling seven properties in just a few years through her agent. Because the agent had talked her out of that first house, my friend trusted her and became totally loyal.

Trust is about being incredibly trustworthy. It's not about trying to gain someone's trust by looking them sincerely in the eye. It's doing what you need to do to serve your clients' best interests. Even if they don't agree with you. It's your fiduciary duty to educate and inform. Obviously, they hold the cards and can make whatever decisions they want, but it's your job to inform them.

You need to trust your gut and walk away when you need to. I once had a client who had bed bugs and refused to disclose it. He claimed he was "just kidding," but I let him know that I could not sell his house as I knew he really did have bed bugs in the past. I couldn't prove it and I couldn't get him to fire me, so I was stuck with him contractually. He was one of the worst clients I've ever worked with: calling, texting, and e-mailing at all hours of the day and night. He was the rudest, most disrespectful person I have ever encountered. He even had the nerve to tell me that I was too busy for him (after his 15th phone call that day and 38th email) while I was at my grandmother's funeral. I calmly let him know where I was, and he *still* proceeded to call and text. He was abusive and impossible to please. I should have smelled him coming, but I had an ego and thought, "I'm going to be the Realtor® that shows this guy. I'm going to overcome his attitude and make him happy."

With my experience, I should have known. All the signs were there. It was the worst experience I've ever had in real estate. He tortured all parties involved which, of course, made me look bad. He even had the nerve to give me a bad review on Zillow and Yelp! I should have paid attention to the red flags. He literally took up more time and energy than the other twenty-seven closings I had during the sixty days I was dealing with him. Now I think of that experience when any red flags come up in my interview process. Never again!

And don't be tempted to fudge a little bit, even if you see it in the industry. It is *not* necessary for your success. In fact, it comes back to bite those who engage in it. We especially saw a lot of shady dealings during the market crash several years ago. Homeowners were desperate and confused, and agents took advantage of that fact. For example, even though with a little work on their part, agents could have sold underwater homes for closer to their prior value, they (with the bank's approval) still would set prices that were $75,000 *lower* just to get the sale done quickly or to bring in their own buyer and double-end the deal. This obviously hurt the homeowner and also devalued the whole neighborhood and the surrounding community. When I was working with short sales, I pushed for the highest prices I could get. Homeowners knew I was watching out for their best interests and my community respected it.

Another way agents took advantage during that time was by flipping houses that were in trouble. Flipping a house is perfectly legitimate, but not when the seller's agent manipulates the deal to the owner's disadvantage. Several agents started getting family members or friends to make offers on a home they had listed. One agent in my area was notorious for this. His brother acted as the buyer and they bought properties for significantly less than their market value. A month later, they would flip them, making thousands of dollars in profit.

This man even took advantage of a woman from his church. She was in the midst of a divorce and underwater on her home, and she asked him for help. Even though she really wanted to stay in the home because of her kids, he convinced her that she wouldn't be able to strike a deal with the bank. He bought the house from her for way under market and she ended up homeless. She told me that she would never forget it. "He convinced me to displace my kids from the school and neighborhood they loved, all just to fill his own pocket."

Once the banks realized that this unethical behavior was taking place, they would not allow an agent to purchase a property or benefit from its sale in any way if he had any involvement in the transaction.

In my time working with banks during REO foreclosure days, I worked really hard to show respect and compassion to the people I was dealing with. It was a difficult and sad time for many people, and definitely a heartbreaking side of the business to be on. I knew I could either make the pain worse for these people or try to be as helpful as I could, given the circumstances. About a year ago, a man called me to sell his home. He said, "You worked with a bank that evicted my mom. You were so gracious and took such great care of her during that time, I will forever be in debt." It was touching. I hated doing that, but I was so glad that his mom's file was given to me to handle so I could show her compassion as she exited the home she had raised her children in.

Look, you don't need to work the system. As a Community Market Leader, doing all the things a Community Market Leader does, you'll have plenty of clients and make all the money you want. And you'll sleep well at night.

Take the Next Step

1. *Go to the example branding and avatar worksheets in the Resources section at the back of the book. Use these to start creating your brand and niche.*

2. *Grab a piece of paper and write "The Business I'd Love to Have" at the top. Without censoring yourself or worrying about how you'll get there, write down how your perfect business would look.*

Be sure to visit **www.sell100homesbook.com** for free resources that will help you grow and automate your real estate business.

CHAPTER THREE

Go Above and Beyond for Your Clients

Let's start with how a traditional broker deals with a listing client: He gives a price to the client (hopefully within the realm of reasonable!) Or worse, lets the client set the price. The broker then has the client sign the listing agreement in a zillion places, spending just a few seconds to explain each page. Or, he may even let the client sign it online with no explanation at all. He then tells the seller to get the house "show ready," snaps a couple of photos, puts the house on broker tour, and throws the listing on MLS and maybe on Zillow. He puts up a lawn sign, maybe even with a packet of flyers. Next—wham!—he sets up an open house! Woo hoo! And for the next few weeks, the client hears little or nothing from the broker unless he has a viable prospect in hand.

I'm not saying that everyone is that bad. Many agents put more effort into their work and do a better job. But a Community Market Leader really goes above and beyond, using traditional tools in innovative ways and employing new tools. They don't do the same old, same old. They don't do the minimum they can get away with.

First of all, even if you're brand new in the business, you know that an open house does *absolutely nothing* for the client. The only thing an open house is good for is gaining leads for the broker. It attracts looky-loo neighbors and a few people who are driving around bored on a Saturday who may, someday, want to buy a house. Still most traditional brokers continue to use them. Open houses help agents meet the neighbors who might be thinking of selling and attract brand new buyers who aren't yet working with an agent or who aren't pre-approved, or if they were approved, the approval wouldn't be in the price range of the open house. Let's face it, real buyers are working with an agent, looking at houses in their price range, on their own time schedule. Not going to open houses.

Just recently a co-worker asked if he could do an open house with one of my listings. I told him how I felt about open houses and that I always tell my sellers how I feel about them. But if he wanted to do one and the seller would allow it, by all means, go ahead and waste a Saturday. So, he did. During this open house, two groups of people came in at the same time. He could tell something fishy was going on. The people all split up and he found one of the women rummaging through the jewelry box that had been hidden in the closest. He was mortified. As the people were leaving, a bracelet fell from the woman's pocket onto the floor. He was really upset, and called the police and his clients. Needless to say, the open house wasn't a big hit. He ended up with no buyers and very stressed out sellers.

The average agent glosses over the whole process of selling a home with little explanation to his clients. Selling their home is a big deal for clients and one of the most important financial decisions they'll make. The paperwork is confusing and most folks have no idea what "show ready" even means. They want to know what's going on as their house is on the market and how well it's being received. They actually want to help with getting their home sold if they can. Some agents almost consider clients as a "nuisance" they have to put up with, not a valued partner.

You know how the average agent operates. So, let me show you how a Community Market Leader handles a listing. This is what I used to call my 60 Point Marketing Plan. It still has over 60 steps to it, but I've simplified it for client presentations. I send this piece to prospective clients before our listing appointment, then I explain it to them so they see *exactly* what I'll provide to them—and I close around 93% of all my listing appointments.

Here's the step-by-step process I've developed that has kept me in the Top 1% in my county for over sixteen years. (No matter what the economy is doing or what market conditions we're in, I still have remained in the top 1% nationally, as well.) As you read through the process, don't panic! I'll give you more detail about how I do each step later in this chapter. And you certainly don't have to implement every single step from the get-go. Implement a few pieces at a time. Get comfortable with them and add your own personality and ideas. Then incorporate a few more steps. (I focus on listings, not buyers. However, we have similar processes for buyers that I'll share in the next chapter.)

Krista Homes 60 + Marketing Digital Platform

Here is the copy from our brochure that tells prospective clients *exactly* what we'll do for them:

Client Care and Communication

We'll be your partner as we work together to get you the best price in a timely fashion. We're confident we can earn your trust and our policy is:

You can cancel at any time if you aren't **100% Satisfied** with our work!

As your partner, we offer our expertise to help you make good decisions about the sale of your home and avoid costly mistakes. It starts with making sure your home is presented to its best advantage:

- 360 Degree Picture Virtual Walk Through of the home
- I-Guide photography which gives exact specific measurements, floor plans, room sizes, etc. Online website feature with added benefits
- Floor Plans and measurements both inside and out
- In-depth analysis and expert advice on pricing strategy for optimal results
- Free consultation with professional Home Designer / Stager
- Free basic staging with Professional Home Designer/ Stager
- Professional staging services, as needed, to attract buyers (optional full staging available at extra charge)
- Free Digital Marketing Specialist to maximize online presence
- Checklist of recommended changes to your home to ensure optimal pricing
- List of reputable vendors for any work required
- Meeting with Marketing Specialist to identify your home's upgrades and features that you, as the homeowner, find important
- Synched lock box to track Realtor® showings and elicit feedback the next business day, which is then sent to you to keep you in the loop

While we market your home, we know you want to be informed and involved. To keep communications flowing, we'll:

- Send a report on our marketing efforts and results twice per week
- Inform you of any market changes, mortgage rate fluctuations, sales trends, absorption rate, or any other factors that may affect the value or marketability of your home

- Provide you marketing materials to share with your neighbors, connections, and on your personal Facebook page and other social media sources (Twitter, LinkedIn, Instagram, etc.)

High-Quality Marketing Materials

The quality of marketing materials representing your home have a huge impact on how it is perceived in the marketplace. To position your home in its best light, we provide:

- Professional photographer to capture interior and exterior images
- Professional videography to create a high definition 2 to 4-minute virtual property tour with description of your home
- Drone Photography
- A high quality, full color four-page brochure featuring your home
- An individual property website which includes:
  o printable brochures
  o photo gallery
  o virtual tour
  o property map
  o reports for out of town buyers showing nearby amenities, school scores and distance, community information, city demographics, and a "contact me" button
- Luxurious lawn sign with solar lighting, our highly recognizable Homes by Krista logo, and a customized texting feature directed to your home's website
- Search engine optimization (SEO) of all marketing materials by Digital Marketing Specialist for maximum online exposure

- All materials cell phone compatible (91% of buyers use cell phones in their home search according to National Association of REALTORS®)
- Online mortgage calculator to help buyers decide if they can afford to purchase your property (website and mobile app)

Tapping the Power of Social Media and the Internet

A recent NAR report states that real estate activity on social media has dropped—but that's because most agents do not understand how to use it effectively. Using our process, we get thousands of hits and shares per month. Your home will be exposed to a broad—yet targeted—audience by:

- Pre-market information to potential buyers currently searching with "Coming Soon" campaign on various social media and internet sites
- Marketing to over 650,000 agents, to 15 countries in 19 languages
- Virtual property tour added to our YouTube channel with description crafted to enhance search engine optimization
- Boost Target Market paid advertisement on social media featuring the property tour video, which typically generates over 50,000 + views, comments, likes, and shares
- Creating cookies on the backend of the marketing to capture and create a target audience
- Online syndication that includes Realtor.com, Zillow, Trulia, Facebook, YouTube, Twitter, Craigslist, Homes By Krista, Oodle, HotPad, Backpages, and Oolx with weekly posts and updates to keep your home in top spots
- Paid listing enhancements to keep your property in prime position on these sites

- Back end access to major real estate sites to create unique, attractive postings that are more accurate than MLS information
- Paid ads through Adwerx (Adwerx technology identifies and analyzes online consumer behavior to target potential buyers looking in your area, even if they are hundreds of miles away)
- Weekly Facebook ad campaign exclusively to people who are categorized with a "Likely to Move" residential profile per Facebook analytics
- Instagram posts about your home to reach the millennial market
- Contests and giveaways on social media promoting your home's virtual tour
- Virtual tour and photos on www.KristaHomes.com with description written to enhance search engine optimization
- Constant analysis of online traffic data to tweak your campaign to increase traffic and conversion rates
- Craigslist ads posted locally and out of the area twice per week.
- Immediate follow-up to online interest or inquiries by phone or by sending video response via text or email
- Target market potential buyers to determine who is the most likely buyer willing to pay the highest price both locally and out of the area
- Twitter
- LinkedIn

Engaging the Real Estate Community

Through our massive online and social media campaigns, we access thousands of buyers directly. But, we also take pains to engage the real estate community:

- Cooperate with all Real Estate companies in Contra Costa County and surrounding counties using multiple MLSs
- E-flyers sent to local and out of area agents with Bar Code feature that brings them directly to your home's website
- Promote your property directly to the top 100 Realtors® in all 3 surrounding counties (Contra Costa, San Joaquin, and Alameda)
- Contact preferred lenders for any prospective buyers in their network
- Email "Just Listed" e-flyer with links to your home's website to thousands of local affiliates and partners in our database
- Announce home to our national network of real estate agents
- Send property specific information to our internal buyers' agents who receive hundreds of inquiries monthly
- Contact agents to request feedback after home is shown, which we then forward to you
- Perform a reverse prospecting search to identify prospective buyers in MLS

Traditional Marketing on Steroids

Though we are experts at online and social media marketing, we don't ignore traditional methods that are still effective. In our campaign, we also:

- Send direct mail and email flyers about your home to our database of clients

- Contact Homes By Krista leads, centers of influence (i.e. family, friends, community leaders), and past clients for potential buyers

- Mass mail an 8 ½ by 11 colored glossy "Just Listed" post card to approximately 500 to 1,000 people in your specific neighborhood

- Hand deliver high quality, 4-page colored brochures to 100 immediate neighbors with a "Pick Your Neighbor" letter attached and text feature

- 4-page colored brochures featuring your home's highlights

- Mass mail "Just Listed" cards to your neighborhood and target areas with multiple homes

- Send mass mailers with your home and other available properties to local neighborhoods, approximately 30,000 sent once per month

- Hire a service to make calls to surrounding neighbors promoting the features and lifestyle benefits of your home

Behind the Scenes

While all this activity is happening, we're also working behind the scenes to make sure your home gets the most exposure so it sells at the best price in a timely manner. We gather all information necessary to ensure a smooth transaction. To that end, we:

- Immediately send video responses to buyer leads via e-mail and text

- Improve the marketing of any under-performing marketing campaigns by analyzing and viewing results of campaigns

- Meet weekly with the team to keep on top of each step in the marketing campaign of your home
- Price the property correctly the first time to widen the window of buyer showings
- Reassess pricing if online traffic is not converting into offline tours
- Answer any questions that arise throughout the transaction via our full staff of specialists
- Use infra-red technology of Supra Lockbox to monitor agent showings to get fast feedback
- Research ownership and deed type from Title Company
- Research property's current land use, zoning, deed restrictions, and easements
- Research tax records to verify full and complete legal information is available to prospective buyers and buyer's agent on MLS printout
- Verify that your property is free of all liens

Once the sale of your home is pending, we stay proactive, not reactive, to make sure the process goes smoothly and efficiently by:

- Verification with agent and lender to ensure buyer is properly qualified, ready, and able to purchase (verified employment, reviewed taxes, bank statements, credit report, 1003, etc.) *before* accepting the offer
- Bi-weekly communication via e-mail about status and progress of sale
- Text message and e-mail reminders to you about appointments and deadlines of escrow, seller disclosures, buyer inspections, appraisal report, buyer final walk through, signing loan documents, and final closing documents

- Constant communication with cooperating side agent and lender to give accurate feedback to seller about status of loan and escrow

Let me ask you: **Do you know of anyone in the business who is doing even *half* that much for each and every listing client?** I'm guessing not.

Before I break it all down for you, let me just share a few thoughts about commission. I charge a higher commission than anybody else because I give more value than anyone else. Right now, the standard commission in my area is 4½% to 5%, and some agents are even taking less. No one charges 6%, so I charge 5½%. I take 3%, and I give 2½% to the buyer's broker.

As I write this, we are in a seller's market. If we were in a buyer's market, I would charge 6% and I would give 3% to the buyer's side to incentivize them. I would take 3% and *still* provide my clients with the same services. I do it this way because I know, in a buyer's market, offering a higher commission to the buyer's agent will ensure the house gets shown more. I end up with quicker sales, which creates happier clients, which equates to more money and more listings. By the way, out of that higher commission I charge, 100% of the extra ½% goes to marketing, basic staging, and mass marketing of the property so it shows in its best light.

Do my clients squawk about the higher commission? Nope. They can see how much more value I provide compared to the average agent. I'm basically setting a new standard of what it means to be a Realtor® in our area. People come to me because they recognize the difference between what I'm doing and what others do. Clients deserve that, they should expect it, and they get it from me. My products and services are unique, so my clients do not balk at the commission. They see the value in what I do. Last year I sold my homes at prices that averaged 2.6% *higher* than my competitors. (Do the math. That covers almost all my commission.)

You need to go above and beyond, and *show* your clients the value you're providing—even the money you'll spend to make sure they end up with the best result. The more you do that, the more your clients are going to boast about you and appreciate you. Neighbors see the same value and they notice that you're different. Your high-quality brochures are dropped off at their houses. They see you plastered on social media, marketing houses in their neighborhood. When it's time for those neighbors to sell, they'll automatically think of you and call. Many times I walk into a house and they pull out some great marketing piece I did years ago. "I kept this because it was so different and nice. I'd never seen one like this, so I thought to myself, 'When I sell I'm going to call her.'"

You want your clients to be so thrilled by your service that they are boasting about you even before they have an offer. Here's how you make sure that happens:

Client Care and Communication

Some agents treat clients as if they aren't really a part of selling their homes. These agents get the listing agreement signed, then bench their clients for the duration until they need to show up to sign closing papers. Big mistake. Your clients not only want to be involved, they can make a huge contribution to how successful the sale is—*if* you communicate with them effectively.

To me, real estate is second nature so it took me a while to understand that communicating isn't just telling my clients about the process. It's taking the time to make sure they understand it. I talk fast, which is okay, but I needed to learn to speak slowly enough so people can keep up with me. And I had to break it all down and explain the process like I did when I was teaching third graders. Not that my clients aren't smart. They might know everything about aerospace or medicine or running a restaurant. But when it comes to real estate? You need to break it down step by step, piece by piece.

Real estate has its own lingo and its own way of doing things, and it changes constantly. Your clients only deal with real estate when they buy or sell their home. How often is that? If I wanted to be an electrician, I wouldn't have a clue about how to be an electrician, or what electricians say or do. But if someone broke it down step by step, really took the time and articulated it so I could understand, I would be able to get it.

Let's take something as simple as telling a client to "get your house show ready." To some people, show ready means making the bed, putting dishes in the dishwasher, and flushing the toilet. The process is much more involved than that. It means opening all the windows, making sure all the lights are on, making sure the house is at a good temperature, making sure personal pictures are removed, and making sure the clients—and their pets— are not present. And this is just the tip of the iceberg! Unless you have specifically told them everything they need to do (or better yet, left them with a checklist), how could they know all that? You could easily spend half an hour breaking down every piece of what "being show ready" means. And, they still might not remember everything you tell them.

I create videos for my clients to remind them of what's expected during every phase. They forget what we tell them. We're often so caught up in doing our jobs, we forget that what comes so easily to us isn't that easy for them. Often they will smile and nod, but once you walk out that door, the questions start flowing. They forget or didn't quite understand the terminology. They are bombarded with a lot of information all at once. They feel a certain amount of anxiety about the whole process.

Have you ever gone into a doctor's office where you're given a serious diagnosis of some kind? Even if it isn't life-threatening, your brain is so busy trying to absorb what it means to your life that you miss 80% of what the doctor tells you about it. If your doctor is good and breaks it down, you might think you understand. But as soon as you hit home and someone asks you about it, you realize that you don't fully understand what the doctor said or what comes next. It's the same with our clients.

I recently went with one of my best friends who was diagnosed with breast cancer to appointments with her doctors. She was meeting with a medical team to find out what her options were. Her husband was with her and she was beyond stressed and scared. It all happened so quickly. They are both incredibly smart. My friend's husband is a teacher and she is a Director of Human Resources for one of the largest school districts. When we walked out of that meeting, both she and her husband had misunderstood most of what they were told. Though I was worried for my friend, my emotions weren't as heightened as theirs. I was on alert and knew I had to listen carefully and take notes. I was able to clarify what the doctors had said.

Sellers and buyers feel like my friend and her husband. According to a poll from dailymail.com, buying a house is more stressful than bankruptcy, divorce, and even the death of a loved one.

Sellers and buyers don't know what they don't know. In my area, buyers' agents call the seller directly to arrange a showing. Some clients assume that you as listing broker will show the property to potential buyers. If you haven't explained how it works to the client, they can get freaked out when some broker they don't know calls them to walk around their home with a potential buyer in tow. If you explain it to them ahead of time, it's fine. If you don't, they start to wonder what the heck is going on.

Instead of repeating every the in and out of selling my clients' homes in person, I use the series of short videos I created that teach them all they need to know. Rather than spending a ton of my time, I send these videos via email so they can watch them at their convenience. I do this throughout the life cycle of their time with me in every phase. And of course, clients can call me if they have questions. I've used those client questions to update and improve my videos.

108

For example, I have a video called, *What to Expect Next*. It reminds clients that the stager will be contacting them and that we will be arranging for video and photographs. Another video reminds them of what they need to do to prepare for the appraiser and home inspector, including making sure the smoke detectors are working, the water heater is strapped properly, and that they have a CO_2 alarm. I have another video that goes into contingencies, what they mean and when they are due to be removed.

I have one video called *Seller Beware* that warns them about all the weird things that happen when agents start showing their house: People won't show up for their appointment. They'll use your bathroom and leave it messy. They'll lock the door you normally enter and leave closet doors and cupboards open.

I also warn them about what to say and what *not* say to buyers' agents. It may sound like chit chat, but agents will ask inappropriate questions to get a competitive edge. "How many offers do you have? Why are you moving? Are you presenting offers as they come in? What does my client need to do to get your home?" **All of these questions should be going directly through me**. Often sellers don't know this and they have no idea how their answers can be used against them. I kid you not, these types of questions get asked all the time. It's inappropriate and if I didn't properly inform my sellers about what to say and not say, they'd spill their guts like a parishioner in confessional.

Another important video I send out explains what "closing" means and what to bring to the closing (I.D., bank routing number, driver's license, etc.) They are reminded to read through their paperwork ahead of time and jot down any questions.

My videos help the seller feel confident because they know what to expect—and they know I'm on top of it. In fact, throughout the process, *all* my communications with clients aren't traditional emails. I also use some video emails. It stands out, feels more personal, and makes a difference in how well they absorb the information.

As we discussed in Chapter Two, these video emails can be either standardized, made once then automated or, if they are specific to one client, they can be made quickly using your laptop camera.

We start involving our clients with the Seller Homework checklist (you can find this at www.KristaHomes.com), which they get right after they sign the listing. It lets them know they play an important part in the successful sale of their home.

Client Care and Communication has three main categories. Here is more detail about what I do specifically:

Showing the Home to Best Advantage:

In my initial listing appointment, I come armed with in-depth information to show the seller how to create a winning pricing strategy. I don't simply pull out the latest report on comps. That data is not only limited, it's often useless without digging deeper. Did Comp A take months and months to sell because it was filthy and you had to use a machete to get to the front door? Did Comp B have thousands of dollars' worth of upgrades that bumped its price up? Was the seller for Comp C desperate and willing to accept a below market price? Did Comp D take a long time to sell because it wasn't marketed properly? Did Comp E use an out of town agent who didn't know how certain neighborhoods' price points are different due to location? Could Comp F involve a divorce where the owners didn't care about price and just wanted it sold quickly? Without this kind of information—which you can only get by digging and really knowing your market—setting a price using only the CMA does your client a real disservice.

Precision pricing is critical to a successful sale. An overpriced home will get fewer showings, take much longer to sell, and usually requires several price reductions. Most over-priced homes ultimately end up selling for less than if the price was set competitively in the first place. That said, you don't want to leave thousands on the table by underpricing your clients' homes either.

To give your client an accurate assessment of pricing and pricing strategy, you need to study absorption rates, pending sales, market climates, interest rates, and inventory levels. All of these factors, and many more, can affect pricing. It's important that you know about all of them and advise your clients properly. Educate yourself and your clients, be aware of what's happening locally and nationally, and how it may affect your sellers and buyers.

In this first interaction with potential clients, it's critical to manage expectations. Though you want the seller to list with you, don't make the mistake of inflating the price or telling them their home will sell faster than you sense it will. You'll be setting yourself up to fail and leave a trail of very unhappy clients behind you. Instead, without being pessimistic, warn clients of any potential landmines. For instance, are lenders lending less and requiring stronger qualifications? That means fewer potential buyers. Does the economy look shaky? People will be less likely to make a major financial move like buying a new home. Show your potential clients that you really care about their success by giving them as much information as you can.

In this first meeting, I also give sellers my recommendations of work that will help the house show better. It may be as simple as having the windows washed, the house thoroughly cleaned, and the carpets shampooed to get rid of pet odor. It might be more extensive, like updating kitchen cabinets or removing a wall. If they've had ideas about pre-sale work they want to do on the house, we discuss that as well. I talk to the sellers about which improvements might be worth it and why, taking into consideration market conditions and their expectation from the sale. I don't wait until they've signed the listing agreement to have this discussion, as many agents will. To me, it is important that clients have all the facts upfront rather than finding out three months into the listing what they could have done in the beginning to help sell their home.

To help them with any improvements they decide to make, I keep lists of contractors and vendors who have shown themselves to be reliable, efficient, and cost effective. I don't just give them the cheapest contractors in town, but the ones I've fully vetted who do excellent work.

The average agent might give clients tips on how to make their homes more attractive and marketable. But how much does that help compared to professional staging? A survey of Realtors® by the NAR said that professional staging can increase a home's sale price by 6% to 10%. And, according to an AOL Financial article, staged homes sell approximately 17% faster. I've run into other research that shows homes sell for around 6% higher with professional staging. Though these statistics may be a little high, isn't it worth it to you and your client to consider staging?

The National Association of Exclusive Buyer Agents (NAEBA) also surveyed brokers and agents. The professionals surveyed said that 82% of home buyers are less focused on any negatives in the home when it is staged. These buyers not only fall in love with the house, but they are willing to pay more, sometimes overpaying. Obviously, we aren't trying to hide anything and we fully disclose any issues the house has. But why not take the emphasis off negative issues and showcase its positives?

Even if your client has a knack for decorating, it doesn't mean they understand staging. I provide my clients with 6-10 hours of professional staging consultation for free (actually, I give them as much time as needed). I pay the consultant $45 per hour out of my own pocket (you can find stagers for as low as $20 per hour) and it makes a huge difference. My stager meets with the client within 24 hours of signing the listing agreement. At this meeting, she goes over what they can do so the house shows better. She tells them where to position furniture so a room looks more inviting. She makes sure closets aren't too overloaded and removes personal pictures. She shows the clients how far to open blinds and how to arrange drapes. She exchanges a painting for a mirror, or removes a table extension to make the table look smaller and the room look bigger.

We bring in our own pictures, knick-knacks, and towels to place throughout the home to give it a fresh, updated look. I store all the items I've bought in a barn and I've added to it over the years. You can go to Home Goods, Kirklands, or Ross to pick up great products to use. You'd be amazed at just how much this small effort adds to the attractiveness of a home. Your investment in props doesn't have to be huge, and my props are always reused. I buy things that are very neutral, whites and beiges, that can be used anywhere.

After this first consultation, the stager comes back and brings the prop pieces she'll be using. It might be knickknacks or towels for the bathroom. It might be dishes or baskets for the kitchen, or throws for the living room. She spends time making sure everything looks great. Only then do we arrange for professional photos and video.

I also give clients the option to pay for more extensive staging. This might entail bringing in furniture or even repainting a wall or two. Depending on the home, this might be worth it to them.

After the stager is done, my marketing specialist and my digital marketer meet with the client. My marketing specialist digs for any upgrades or improvements clients have made to their homes. She asks them what they love about their house and their neighborhood. My digital marketer is the person who does all our online marketing and who designs our online pieces (such as landing pages, social media posts, target market ads) for search engine optimization (SEO). This SEO work means the difference between a posting that gets a few dozen hits versus one that gets thousands. My digital marketer and marketing specialist take note after note about every single detail of the property so we can market it effectively.

Our online digital platform is unbeatable and has been built from extensive research and training classes. My digital marketer and I recently attended Nicholas Kusmich's class, "The Art of Lead

Generation." This was a 2-day course that taught us how to run target market Facebook campaigns. The class fee alone was $6,500 and, with travel and food, it cost me just under $10,000—but it was well worth every penny. These types of trainings and classes are what keep my business on the cutting edge so I can give the most value to my clients. It makes me feel great about what I do and how I serve them.

Informed and Involved:

As soon as our marketing materials are ready, we shoot copies (hard copy and electronic) to our clients so they can post them on their Facebook pages and other social media outlets, such as Instagram and LinkedIn, and hand them to friends, or send them out in emails. Think about it: People usually know a lot of people who are similar to themselves in income level, likes and dislikes, maybe even profession. The people who will be most interested in their home are most likely those people who are like the sellers. Tapping their area of influence only adds to your pool of potential buyers—and potential clients.

When the house is on the market, the average agent might make a phone call once or twice per week to check in. But clients don't just want you to "check in." They want real information about what's going on. The lock box on the home is registered so we know who goes in and out. Each time a property is shown by another agent, we ask for specific property feedback so we can relay it to the seller. We do this the next business day after the showing and we blind copy the seller when making the request to the showing agent so they see we are requesting it. Then we forward the agent's feedback once we get it back (which is about 45% of the time and we let our clients know that's typical).

My clients hear from us at *least* twice per week while the house is on the market. Twice per week, we send them the new print or digital marketing material we've created or the most recent postings on various sites. We set up systematic calls on specific days every week to update them on activity. We tell them how many postcards we've sent, how many brochures we've hand-delivered, and a list of new postings on websites. They also get a run down on how many showings the house has had. We do formal video updates for our clients through BombBomb each week. We also include them on our weekly market update and education list so they get that video every week as well.

What do we get in return? Clients who are excited and referring other people to me even before we've sold their home. They are clear about all the efforts we are making on their behalf and they trust that *I* know what I'm doing. If, for some reason, the house isn't selling as quickly as they'd hoped, they know it is not because we are not doing everything we can. If I were only holding an open house and sending out a few flyers rather than not doing all of this, I would be stressed out if the home wasn't selling. Keeping your client informed and showing them that you are doing everything you can takes the heat off. It is also how you earn your full commission without discounting.

High-Quality Marketing Materials

Let me say this again: the quality of your marketing material reflects both on the quality of the home *and* the quality of your own work. Typical agents pull out their iPhones, snap a few shots, and call it good. Their "video tours" are just slide shows of the photos they took. Their flyers are cheap throw-aways that are more self-promotional than designed to really feature the house. Don't do that.

After the home is staged to look its best, we bring in a professional photographer and a videographer. They don't have to be highly expensive. You can find talented college kids or people on Craigslist and Fiverr. Unless you yourself have done a lot of photography, they'll know more than you about lighting and how to use angles of shots to make something look more impressive. If you don't have the money right now, make your own iPhone video, but then spend $15-$20 to have Fiverr edit it for you. You can do anything less expensively and still do it well. Use a drone for footage if you have access to drone photography. Use the drone shot as the first picture on MLS and marketing sites. It will draw attention to the home and to you. Again, it's about being unique and going above and beyond.

Let's talk about creating the website I use for listings. I don't mean a slideshow on your company's website with a few facts about the home. We put together a robust website for each home that is separate from my company's website. For one hundred dollars per month, you can create as many individual property websites as you want with a bunch of features. For example, the site can forward emails and has a "chat" feature that will notify your cell phone of the inquiry so you can text back. On each of these websites, we have the slideshow and virtual tour of the property, a detailed description, a mortgage calculator (so buyers can calculate whether they can afford the payments), nearby amenities and schools, local demographics, and an aerial street view. The site can be accessed by computer, cell phone, or any mobile device.

Interested buyers can contact us using the text number on the home's lawn sign or on our other marketing materials. When a text comes in, we respond automatically and send the URL for the home's website right to the interested buyer's mobile phone. (We also automatically text the URL to buyers who show interest on Zillow and other sites.) Best of all, when they use the texting feature, the software will text and email me their contact info and what property they are inquiring about. When an interested buyer lands on the site, the site also collects their information so we can follow up with them quickly.

This is the place where search engine optimization comes in and understanding optimization methods on specific property marketing sites like Zillow, Realtor.com and Trulia becomes critical. You can create an awesome website, terrific YouTube ads, and dynamite Craigslist ads. But if you ignore how each specific site tells you to optimize your listing to get it to show up and stand out, you're wasting your time.

For those of you who aren't familiar with SEO, it's basically the way people find you online. When you Google something like "homemade toothpaste," the search engines hunt for words that most closely match what you want to find. SEO figures out what words people use most often to find whatever you have. So, in our example, statistics might show that words like "natural," "teeth," "toothpaste," and "homemade" are the words people most often put in that search box. With SEO, you take that information and make sure that your descriptions and titles use the most popular words so your product will pop up on the first page. Using the correct words to describe your videos, websites, and online ads will ensure you have higher ranking in the search engines and that your target market will find you. This applies to Facebook, social media target market specific ads, and anything you put online. (There is a lot of technology and information behind SEO and it could take up an entire chapter in itself. One quick hint is to make sure you add a title to all of your pictures.)

We also go into the back end of the top websites, such as Zillow, Realtor.com, Trulia, and Redfin. (These are the top sites currently, but that can change overnight. It's technology!) By getting into the back end of our listings, we can enhance our copy to get better exposure, and we can analyze how well our post on that site is performing. We create cookies to re-target viewers, saving marketing dollars by being more specific about who sees our marketing.

Basically, a cookie is a tracking link that follows buyers and sellers online so when they click on our ads, posts, websites or links, they start to automatically get our future listings, videos, and updates. Don't freak out! This is so simple that anyone can do it. You'll just need a little training. Using cookies will create a "Target Audience"

Latest Activity

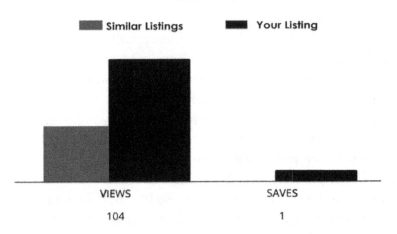

Your Listing is doing GREAT!
4 days on Zillow

███ Similar Listings   ███ Your Listing

VIEWS
104

SAVES
1

Views on your listing this week

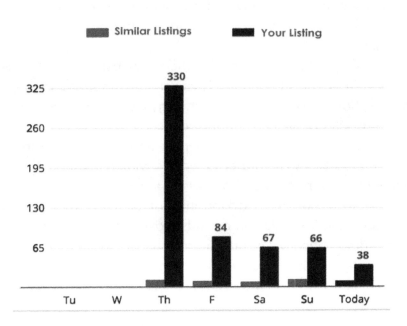

███ Similar Listings   ███ Your Listing

or "Look Alike" audiences who will see all your material organically so you don't have to pay to track them.

More exposure helps the seller's home sell more quickly. I show prospective clients this graph at my listing appointments so I get the two-fold benefit from working the back end of listings: 1) to show my current clients how well their ad is performing during their regular updates, and 2) to impress my prospective clients at a listing appointment.

In terms of other marketing materials, what about something as mundane as your lawn sign? How many agents still use the sign they used fifteen years ago? Same old photo and just a phone number with no website URL or text number. And, unless they've been able to put it under a street lamp, the sign goes totally dark when the sun goes down. How often do you replenish the brochures you put with your sign? (Better yet, how about using a digital brochure or flyer instead so potential buyers can look at the home's information by texting the number on the sign?

If you want quality marketing materials, you will have to spend more than the average agent spends. But it doesn't have to break the bank. When implementing some of these ideas or ideas you come up with on your own, stop and really think about how you can get the job done cost effectively before you plunge in. As you start to make more money, which you will, start to add and expand. Implement, Improve, Expand, Repeat. Always focus on getting better and better and improving/innovating.

Tapping the Power of Social Media and the Internet

Obviously, I do a lot to tap the power of social media and the internet. If you are just starting in this type of marketing, don't become overwhelmed by it. Take it piece by piece. Your goal is to improve. With every house you sell, add something new and stick with that until you really have it down and are doing it consistently. Implement a new technology that will enhance your listing and exposure. Be innovative and use technologies that show you are different. Once you sell another house you can create a bigger budget for your marketing and add something else. The key is consistency. Once you master and implement an innovation or technology, keep doing it and add more. Don't stop with the first, but add to it. Keep in mind that technologies are changing constantly so you'll need to keep track if something new and improved is out there that can better serve your clients and in turn better serve you.

Some of what I do today seems expensive, like spending $200 on a specific ad campaign on Facebook. But if that ad generates 25,000-75,000 views, to me it's totally worth it. However, I didn't start there. I added the extra investment in my business as it grew.

For each video that I produce—whether it's a general education video or a video specific to one of my listings—I am creating a target audience. I'm showing up wherever they are and redirecting them to what I want my audience to see. You're creating an *audience*, not targeting one person. Anyone who's ever looked at your videos, or anyone who's ever researched you, they all become a part of your target audience. You start showing up on their feed, on their computer—anywhere they go, you're there. Then automatically, you redirect them to see that next thing you want them to see.

In my 60+ Digital Marketing Platform, I mention using an online company called AdWerx. AdWerx basically identifies anyone who does a real estate related search in my area. As soon as that person is identified, my posts start showing up on their feed because of their interest in real estate. My ads keep following them online to get their attention so they'll eventually click on my ad, which takes them to my website then to my featured properties. Because they keep seeing me, my name stays in their minds. This is why people tell me they see me *everywhere*.

Engaging the Real Estate Community

Let me start out by saying that I don't do brokers' tours. They're not really effective and I explain that to my clients. Granted this might differ from market to market. You may feel that they are totally useful and work well. If you can prove that and have success with these tours, by all means continue. But don't mistake a brokers' tour as an activity that stands out. The effectiveness of brokers' tours could change in the future, but my research in this area is suggesting that holding brokers' tours is ineffective for attracting buyers. Buyers typically know more about homes on the market than their agents do. If they are serious buyers, they're like crack monkeys, searching for their dream home every minute online. They usually find the homes they want to see before their agent. Maybe at some point in the future brokers' tours might make sense in promoting a listing. However, in my opinion it doesn't now.

That said, brokers' tours are excellent for getting to know other agents, developing rapport, and checking out your competition. They are especially valuable for new agents. Agents work with agents they like, so getting to know other agents is important, especially the top agents. Often sellers will ask my thoughts about, or experience with, another agent when deciding which buyer's offer to choose. So, it is very helpful to connect with your peers.

I send out "Coming Soon" e-flyers to agents locally and throughout the county so they can see we have a new listing coming up. They can then forward that piece to their clients and it makes that agent look good because it provides their clients with so much information. Another very affordable software is called Proxio. It allows agents to market their listings and the listings of other agents to over 650,000 agents, in 15 countries and in 19 languages. Check out Proxio at www.Proxio.com.

Why do I send these out? About four or five years ago I lost a listing presentation to an agent who worked in a large real estate firm with lots of agents. The size of the other agent's firm was the factor that swayed the seller. Of course, 5% of all agents do 95% of all business, so being in a big firm is irrelevant—but the seller didn't think so.

After that experience, I decided to head that "larger firm" objection off at the pass. I started sending out digital flyers to tap into all agents in all companies, which is how agents in big firms connect with each other. I tell that story on my listing presentations.

I even take it a step further by emailing to top agents within the surrounding counties. When the market was slow or in a buyers' market, I would hand deliver brochures to agents' offices and make face to face contact with top producing agents in the area. But honestly that was only when the market was saturated with listings and I needed mine to stand out. In a regular market, that's unnecessary and a time waster for you. Use your work hours effectively so you'll have more time to do what you love.

Traditional Marketing on Steroids

Whatever you do, make sure you do it with intention and purpose, and in an innovative way. Again, what you do reflects positively or negatively on both you and the home. Don't just throw a cheap tri-fold brochure into a mass mailing to everyone in town and hope it hits someone who cares. Be more intentional than that, and spend a bit more money to make a lot more. Do whatever marketing you choose to do *consistently*. Most agents give up if they don't see an instant return on their investment. They think sending out one post card one time should make a big difference. No, it doesn't! You need to do it regularly to create top of mind awareness. People will throw your materials away and won't even notice one measly post card. But, once they are considering selling or buying, they will remember that they've seen you regularly in their mail box—even more so if they've been seeing you on social media.

The 60+ Digital Marketing Platform talks about what we do on the more "traditional" side. I'll only continue doing something if I can see it works. For example, we send out at least five hundred "Just Listed" and "Just Sold" post cards to the surrounding area that are 8 ½ by 11, color and glossy. They have the texting feature on the card for each specific house, as well as details and a colored picture of the home. I work with a lender who shares in this expense. That lender went from not even being on the map to being in the Top 3 in her company after working with me over the past three years. These things work. Mailings often just get tossed out, but once a homeowner is thinking of selling, they notice them and remember that they've received them regularly. Believe it or not, I've walked into a seller's home and they have drawers full of my postcards. Again, the key is to be consistent and send them on a regular schedule 100% of the time, not just every once in a while. You should always be focusing on Location Domination so you'll send these out to your farm even if the house you are marketing isn't in that area. The key is to get people to constantly see you and see that you're doing business.

Behind the Scenes

Back office activity may not seem exciting enough to impress a potential client—*unless* what you've got going behind the scenes shows the incredible value you'll be providing. When you read through this Behind the Scenes section, you realize that it's a lot more than just administration or shuffling paperwork. To create and maintain a healthy team environment, I highly suggest you read Dale Carnegie's book, *How to Win Friends and Influence People*. I listened to the audio book recently, then sent a copy to my entire staff and told them it was mandatory for them to listen to it or read it. Once they complete the book, I'll give them each $100.00. Why? Because the author is a genius, and I want to make sure my staff and I use the wisdom in this book as the basis for how we treat each and every person we interact with. (While my dad was proofing this, he asked if I'd give him $100.00 to read the book. Yes, Dad, it can help everyone!)

Everything my office staff does is focused on giving epic service. We treat our clients the way they'd be treated in a luxury hotel. We fulfill needs they didn't even know they had. We capture every lead and follow up as if they are the perfect person for our listing, or that they'll be our next awesome client. We focus on being proactive, not waiting until a deal gets shaky, but spotting potential bumps in the road long before they appear. And if the agent on the other side isn't doing her job? We're ready to take care of it.

The systems we have in place and the technology we've adopted allow us to do all of this.

When I do things like Craigslist ads, I add the text message feature so I can respond quickly, if not instantly. When someone texts me, the text feature sends me their phone number and says, "This person just texted about this property."

After every appointment, whether it is with a buyer or a seller, I send that prospective client a card saying, "Thanks so much for the meeting, I really appreciated your time." It's a simple, but gracious gesture. It lets the person know we care and we pay attention to detail. If we do that much after just the first meeting, how much more can they expect from us when they actually become our client? We've already started the relationship off right by giving them valuable information. Now we're adding that personal touch that is so important. Writing the card shows the prospective client that you care enough to take the time to do it. Everything you do is a reflection of how you do business in the future.

Being Proactive for a Smooth Close:

If you're reading this book, you're probably not the average type of listing agent who gets an offer in and presents it based on whatever information the buyer's agent has given him. The average agent then simply adds contingences to the counter offer, giving the buyer time to qualify for a loan. We don't. We make sure the buyer has been truly pre-qualified *before* we ever accept an offer, rather than wasting the seller's time with a buyer who may or may not qualify. I verify pre-qualification by having the lender and agent fill out our Property Questionnaire which asks:

1. Have you verified employment?
2. Have you reviewed current and previous income taxes?
3. Have you looked at bank statements?
4. Did the buyer fill out the entire loan application, including Form 1003? (In California, this form asks deeper questions about past bankruptcies, short sales, foreclosures, child support, etc.)
5. Do you feel comfortable telling me credit scores?
6. Debt to income ratio?
7. Has lender checked for special assessments or higher property tax level and notified buyer, as well as incorporated it into their payment?
8. Have you informed the client not to open any new credit lines or take out any type of loan?
9. Has buyer personally seen the home?
10. Have you made any offers on any other homes?

I also spend time vetting the buyer's agent and lender. I check how long they have been in business, how active they are, and whether they work in real estate full-time. Why? So I can give my client an honest opinion about how the transaction based on their offer would probably go.

Recently, I had eight offers on a property and the sellers asked me which one I would choose. I mentioned that one of the agents said she hadn't had a home *not* appraise for over three years. At that point in time, I was seeing houses not appraise about 3-4 times per *month*. I knew that she hadn't explained to her clients what it meant to remove the appraisal contingency, that they would have to pay the difference between their offer and the appraisal value the lender would use for their loan.

That buyers' agent wasn't worried about the home not appraising because she was from a different market. She wasn't familiar enough with our market to know that prices were increasing so fast that appraisers weren't keeping up with the market. I wouldn't have known about her misjudgment of the situation if I had not personally called and vetted that agent. Fortunately, we didn't take that offer because guess what? Big shocker, the house did *not* appraise, but came in $18,000 under the offer. We had measures in place to protect the seller against the house not appraising so they were able to get their full contract price.

It's not just about the obvious terms of an offer. You need to unearth other aspects of the deal that might make for a bumpy—or failed—transaction. My team and I do all of this research and ask these questions to avoid as many potential issues as we can.

Once the offer is accepted, I have the buyer, buyer's agent, and lender sign a form stating that I am able to contact the lender directly. We stay in constant contact with the lender rather than getting third hand information from the buyer's agent—and we're usually the first to know if something is about to run off the rails. We also call the agent and lender to go-over the questionnaire to be sure they didn't leave anything out that potentially could affect the seller. For example, when we call, we often unearth the fact that the buyer's agent didn't include the contingency that the buyer must sell their prior home before the transaction can close. They figure it's no big deal because that sale was pending. But that is information my seller and I absolutely need to know. How often has a pending sale not closed on time—or at all?

After the offer is accepted, we treat our clients like their doctor's office would treat them, with reminders the day before every appointment via text and email. This doesn't have to be tedious and time consuming. Software can do this easily and generate reminders automatically once you enter the dates. Three days before any contingency deadline, we send the buyer's agent a reminder of their responsibility and offer our help, if needed. All of this is automated via Realvolve so nothing drops through the cracks. It also saves us time.

We not only remind our sellers of their responsibilities, but we make sure they do it right the first time. For example, on the California Association of Realtors® transfer disclosure statement, one of the questions is, "Has anything ever been repaired, replaced, modified, added, fixed or changed in the home?" It's incredible to me, but probably 85% of the disclosures I get from other agents' clients say, "no" to this, even when they've lived in the house for decades. Are you kidding me? You've never fixed a broken faucet or replaced the garbage disposal? You've never needed to have your hot water heater replaced or your garage door repaired? You've never installed new light fixtures?

Obviously, the seller filled the form out by themselves with little or no coaching from their agent. It's the law that those things get disclosed. Being sloppy can open both the seller and the agent to a lawsuit. Instead, I advise my clients to grab a glass of wine and their laptop, and go room to room, really thinking about any work they've had done. What have they repaired? Replaced? Upgraded? You do a disservice to your client if you don't tell them to be thorough. I give my clients examples of what a proper disclosure looks like and add addendums to the contract so they can elaborate on any changes they've made to their home. (We all know how small the lines are on those forms. Using an addendum ensures clients don't leave anything out.)

During this final stage, it's especially important to make sure your client understands what is happening and when. I can't tell you how many past clients thought that when they go to sign the closing documents, they'll be handing over their keys and picking up their check. They're excited—then very, very disappointed. I've learned to make sure they understand the escrow process, especially the timing of this last piece, by sending out another video after offer acceptance that explains it all.

Take the Next Step

1. *Make a list of all the valuable things you do for your clients already. Identify any holes you see in how you're working with clients today. How can you improve and make any deficiencies better?*

2. *Write down 3 ideas from this chapter and schedule a time to implement them in your own business.*

Be sure to visit **www.sell100homesbook.com** for free resources that will help you grow and automate your real estate business.

CHAPTER FOUR

Above and Beyond for
Buyers' Agents

I haven't focused on buyers since my first years in real estate over fifteen years ago. We didn't have as much technology to tap back then, but I still realized that whatever I did had to be innovative so I would stand out from the crowd. I'd hold mass open houses and put fifty signs up. I created an application for buyers to fill out and printed out a ton of relevant information to give to them. I didn't try to sell anyone, but just got to know them and gave them something of value. And it worked. Today I give all my calls from buyers to my buyers' specialists. My buyers' agents need to sell themselves by giving excellent value and educating the buyers as much as possible.

Searching for a new home today is very different than it was fifteen years ago. Heck, it's different than it was just one year ago. Buyers can just go online themselves and research homes for sale. In fact, even if they have an agent, buyers typically know about new houses on the market before their agent does. If they are serious about buying, they're visiting Zillow and Trulia every day searching for a perfect home.

So, the role of a buyers' agent has to change. It's not just that you can find a great home for them. They can do that themselves—though if you stay connected and really know your market, you'll still be able to locate homes that won't show up online. **To be a buyers' agent who adds real value, you need to think differently.** You need to be innovative and give service that is above and beyond the norm. Your goal should be to arm your clients with all the knowledge and resources they need to make a successful purchase.

A CML buyers' agent focuses on these areas:

Intimate Local Market Knowledge: You need an in-depth knowledge of the markets you serve. This includes details, like the area's history and the history of its real estate values, demographics and demographic trends, schools and school ratings, crime statistics, amenities like parks and recreation areas, restaurants and shopping, current and planned commercial development, available transportation and traffic patterns, police and fire stations, available social services, property tax rates, and access to healthcare. I don't mean that you just pick up a report that covers these topics. You want to be as familiar with the area as someone who has lived there for twenty years.

You do a disservice to your buyer if you try to represent them in a market that is far from you or that is unfamiliar to you. If you live 45 minutes away, you won't know the subtle differences between neighborhoods, that the Saturday night high school football crowd echoes through this neighborhood or that neighborhood has a massive number of rental properties. You might miss things like higher tax assessments or that a street is due to be widened.

Part of knowing your areas intimately is having a close relationship with the listing agents in your area and developing a good rapport with them (this is where brokers' tours and attending local agent events can be helpful). As the saying goes, "People like working with people they like." Make an effort to get to know them. Be the kind of agent who is fun and easy to work with. That means being responsive to requests, following up quickly, being prepared, **and dealing fairly, *always*.**

It doesn't mean you should allow yourself to get trampled. But understand that it's more important to be a cooperative player in every transaction than to squeeze every last penny out of it. Building positive professional relationships gives you the inside track. Your offers will be looked upon more favorably because other agents trust and like you. And they will be more comfortable sharing vital information with you.

Thorough Understanding of Your Clients' Goals: A CML buyers' agent goes beyond the typical questions of, "How many bedrooms and baths do you want?" You need to dig and understand your clients' lifestyles and goals, both now and looking down the road into the future. That means finding out where they work and how they feel about commuting, how they like to spend their time at home, what they enjoy doing in their time off, and whether they anticipate their family size changing (having kids, having parents move in with them, getting married, having older kids move out). It covers things like, "Do you have pets and do you walk them every day?" "Do you entertain at home a lot?" "Do you work at night and sleep during the day?" "What amenities are most important to you?" "What hobbies and activities does your family like?" "Is it likely you'll be transferred to another city for work?"

Next, you want to find out specifically *why* your clients decided to buy a house. Are they looking for a forever home or an investment they can turn over in a few years? Is it so their kids can go to a better school? Of all their reasons for buying, which are the most important? By asking all these questions, you not only gain a better understanding of the type of home that will work for them. You're also helping your clients clarify their goals and desires so they can make good decisions. Buying a home is a very emotional step for many people. You want to set your clients up so they don't let their emotions lead them into bad decisions.

The next few steps are about educating your clients. To be efficient, I suggest creating videos of any general information you need to teach them about purchasing a home. Not only will it save you time, but your clients will be able to look back and refer to the videos when they forget what you said. **Keep in mind that what is second nature to you is a confusing jumble of real estate jargon and strange procedures to them.**

The Ins and Outs of Home Ownership: One of the many incredible values you can bring to the table is to educate your clients about home ownership. Owning a home has always been part of the American Dream. But, for people who don't understand the ins and outs of home ownership, it can become a *nightmare*, as we saw in the last real estate crash. The fact that your buyer has owned homes before doesn't necessarily mean they really understand the potential landmines and great benefits of home ownership.

Topics you should cover include things like the impact of market swings on home equity. When the market crash hit, I heard homeowners claim that they'd just lost thousands of dollars on their home. No, they didn't. That "cash" they thought they'd lost was never an actual fact. And, though you used to be able to take built-up equity to the bank and pull it out in a refinance, now it's not as easy to use your home as your personal ATM. Your clients need to understand that, though real estate can be a great investment, its value can go down as well as up.

Calculating How Much Home Can They Afford: You also need to make sure they understand the costs of home ownership including taxes, insurance, utilities, homeowner's association dues, as well as repairs and maintenance. This especially applies to first time buyers and buyers who are moving into larger or more expensive homes than they've owned previously. Find out if they want to include their taxes and insurance in their monthly mortgage payments. It's important to help them factor in *all* the costs they'll incur in owning a home so they can calculate what they can really afford.

Here's a quick checklist of things you should discuss with buyers:

1. Property taxes: In many areas, the sale of a house triggers a property tax reassessment. Research this and warn your clients of possible increases.

2. Lawn and Garden: Help them get an estimate of landscape maintenance charges. Even a basic mow and blow can get costly. If they decide to do it themselves, they'll incur the cost of all the equipment they need. And what about ongoing pest control?

3. "Minor" Upgrades: It's exciting to move into a new house and put your personal stamp on it. But one "small" change invariably leads to another *and* more cost. That new gas stove might require resizing the cabinetry, then repairing floor and counters. Counsel your buyers to be cautious about improvements and suggest they delay them until they've settled in.

4. "Major" Upgrades: A new deck may sound easy and inexpensive, but those projects rarely are. Also, improvements that require getting permits will automatically increase property taxes.

5. General Maintenance: Professional property managers usually create a "reserve for replacement," which is a fund set up for the maintenance issues that will occur: roof repair or replacement, resealing the driveway or re-staining the deck, replacing doors and windows, repair or replacement of furnace and air conditioning—it's a constant flow of issues that need to be addressed. For people who've been apartment dwellers, this can be a huge shock. Let your buyers know that regular, thorough maintenance of their home will directly affect the price they can get when they eventually sell it.

6. Accidents: If the house is on a golf course, your buyers can expect a few balls flying through windows. If they get lots

of deliveries or have lots of guests over, they can expect someone, some time, to drive over their sprinklers or into the garage door. Kids are notorious for throwing things down toilets, putting holes in walls, and breaking doorknobs/lighting fixtures/window blinds/screen doors.

7. Safety: Does that pool need a fence around it? Do those bathrooms need safety handles? Are the stair bannisters sturdy? Will the outside need motion detectors?

8. Emergencies: Does the area tend to flood? If so, what do they need to protect the home? Does power go out frequently due to storms that topple trees? If so, do they need a back-up generator—or at least a bunch of flashlight?

9. Time: One of homeownership's biggest costs is time. If your buyers are "Do It Yourselfers," most of their free time will be eaten up by work on their new home. Even if they hire vendors to do necessary work, they'll spend hours waiting for those vendors to show up.

You can also point out the financial benefits they'll receive in terms of tax write-offs to add to their calculations. When you own a home right now in California, you're able to write off some of the interest, which can save several hundreds of dollars per month and thousands per year. You can either choose to get that money back at the end of the year on your taxes, or you can choose to increase your dependents so you save that money each month. When you factor this benefit in, your clients might be comfortable that they can afford a more expensive home.

The *worst* thing you can do as a buyers' agent is get your clients into a home that they will not be able to afford.

Understanding Financing: You can't just rely on a lender to explain all the options available to your buyers. Spend time to explain to your clients the pros and cons of adjustable versus fixed mortgages, reverse mortgages, interest-only, and 15/20/30 year terms. What are the consequences and benefits of each type of loan, and how will it affect your buyers? Make sure they understand about PMI insurance and impound accounts, if applicable. Mention the benefits of making bi-monthly payments to pay off the home quicker and incur less interest. If you are staying on top of the market, you should know what interest rates they are likely to get and what lenders would be the best match for them. Do they qualify for any special financing?

The financing end of buying a home is incredibly important. Back when the market crashed, a lot of people opted for interest-only loans because mortgage brokers were making so much money by selling those interest-only loans. But, with interest-only, after five years you've never paid anything off the principle. The only people who benefitted from those loans were the mortgage brokers because they made all that money charging excessive points and being paid by the banks to sell high risk loans. Align yourself with good lenders who have the same high ethical standards you have. Make sure they're not in it just for the sale but have a CML® mindset of "people before things."

As far as an adjustable rate, that isn't safe by any means because you never know what can happen. What if rates go up five points? We've all seen this, right? Your clients will have a payment they can afford at one point. Then, five years later, their payment triples and they can't afford the house anymore. Make sure your clients are very clear about their options. Would an extra $200 per month in mortgage payments mean they'd have to cut out parents' date night, fun family outings, or doing the things they really enjoy? Let your clients know, "If extending yourself for your mortgage means sacrificing the things that make your life enjoyable, don't do it! **Don't get shackled to a mortgage payment you really can't afford."** I've seen too many people buy homes they could not truly afford, then lose everything when interest rates sky rocketed. It's devastating!

Also, help your clients position themselves to look good to lenders by showing them how to improve their credit score or suggesting they increase their down payment. Then help them get pre-qualified with a good lender—one that has a good track record and experience—*before* they enter the market. Make sure they get a "to be determined" approval. A TBD pre-approval is fully contracted for the entire underwriting process. All the lender needs is the appraisal to get the loan approved. A TBD is much stronger than a regular preapproval because there are no surprises down the road.

Untangling the Process: Give your clients a *thorough* explanation of everything that happens from submitting an offer to close of escrow. I'd suggest creating a series of videos on this with a checklist to keep track. Cover everything from offers to purchase contracts to contingencies to appraisals. Tell your buyers what to expect from a home inspection or a termite inspection. Help them answer common questions, such as: What happens if the house doesn't appraise? What inspections do they need and is it safe to accept the sellers' inspections? Go into detail and answer all the questions buyers have asked you over the years. Your clients will feel more confident and you'll end up fielding many fewer questions.

As you do this, point out parts of the process that are particular to current market conditions. For example, if you are in a sellers' market, offers have to be more attractive to beat out the competition and get accepted. Buyers may need to move quickly on homes that interest them. They might need to do extras like writing a personal letter to the sellers about what they like about the house and having their lender call the sellers' agent to verify the pre-qualification and the lender's commitment.

As we get into the transaction, we make sure that we give buyers multiple recommendations for inspectors, vendors, carpet repair, window repair—anything they need. We give them multiple references of reputable people and organizations we have good relationships with.

Doing Effective Buyers' Tours: Your job during home tours is not just to be the chauffeur and deal with lock-boxes. You need to think of yourself as the expert your buyers have hired to help them make a great decision on their new home.

Rather than emailing out the standard MLS information on homes you'll be touring, create your own buyers' tour packet. How about a tour package in full color that has additional photos of each house? (See the link to my Buyers' Tour Package in the Resources section.) Leave space for your buyers to take notes and make comments on each home. Include neighborhood information on each home and create a Google map that shows where each house is in relation to others.

Prepare yourself by checking in with sellers' agents to get some background on why the house is selling, how quickly sellers want to move, and whether they'll need to rent back. Dig to understand what is important to the seller. Research the specific location of each home: Are there hazardous waste sites or landfills nearby? Is the home near an electrical plant? Is it near an airport or train tracks? Make notes of these things so you can inform your client about details of the location while on tour.

For example, the traffic is super busy on a couple of streets in my area at certain times because those streets are used as thoroughfares to get to and from school. In the mornings and after school, it's just crazy how busy it is. You would never know about this traffic if you went by the house on a weekend, or if you didn't go by at the right time. A CML® will try to find out that kind of information so there are no unpleasant surprises down the road.

It's just as important for us to point out the negatives of the house as it is the positives. I will let my buyers know, "Hey, I would not buy this because of X, Y and Z" or "This neighborhood is clearly heading downhill." I'm really upfront about future selling and what the resale value of a house would be. Sometimes the negatives are specific to that particular buyer. Somebody else might not mind whatever it is. But, from what they've told me, I know my buyers wouldn't be happy. So, I point out the issues, even if it means I won't get a sale—and you should, too.

If you're doing your job and showing them as many good possibilities as possible, your buyers will have a hard time remembering every house they see. Help them out by making a custom report of each tour. As you tour through each house, use your laptop or iPad to take videos and record your buyers' comments. I use Evernote (an app on my iPad), which allows me to send the notes, pictures, and video digitally, or it can be printed if my clients prefer that. Though you may not be a certified home inspector, pay attention to any indications of possible physical issues in the house, like ceiling stains or foundation cracks. Add your notes to the video and send this to your buyers after the tour to jog their memories. This can be done right in Evernote while you are visiting each property.

Design a Win-Win Offer: When your client has found the house they want, you need to create the strongest offer possible. Is "the strongest offer" the one that guarantees they get the house? No. *The strongest offer is the one that gets them the house on terms that really work for your buyers.* Your buyers might be frothing at the mouth over a certain house. Your job is to help reign in their emotions and ensure that they are happy with their decision two months or a year from now.

You need to be creative and have excellent negotiation skills to make this happen. You have at least twenty deal points to work with. You need to know what the traditional fees are in that county. You need to know what's negotiable, what's customary regarding closing costs, who pays for title, who pays for escrow, who pays for inspections, who pays for the home warranty, what repairs you should actually request or not request, and who is paying the broker fees. Remember that what is customary is always affected by market climate. Everything is negotiable depending on what the market is doing, so set your buyers' expectations up correctly from the beginning. For example, in some counties the buyer pays for all the closing costs, but in others they are split 50/50. Knowing your market and the market norms in an area you're working is essential so your buyers understand and know what to expect, giving them the ammunition they need to create an attractive offer that will be accepted.

Get as much seller information as you can to understand their hot buttons and figure out what leverage you have. Why are they selling? Are there any hardships involved? Look at how many days the home has been on the market. Has the home fallen out of escrow? Why? How many offers are in and how strong are they? Ask the selling agent, "Are you going to respond to all offers or only counter the best?" Make sure your buyer knows when it's a competitive situation and when it's not. Help your buyer understand the differences. If you're in a seller's market, let them know they'll need to show all the strength they've got from the beginning and not leave anything to chance.

Show your buyer how economic indicators, interest rates, real estate cycles, and market conditions, both locally and nationally, play into the offer. For example, in my market right now, homes for first-time buyers are going like hot cakes and we expect multiple offers. I just listed a house last weekend and we had fourteen offers by Monday! In this type of market, you need to let your buyers know, "Hey, they're going to get multiple offers. It's going to go for twenty to thirty thousand dollars above list price, and it's probably not going to appraise." Then you need to talk about the pros and cons of making an offer on that home. Being in a buyers' market versus a sellers' market will drastically impact how you approach the offer, buyer, other agent, and the seller.

Educate your clients about the process and what types of things they should or should not request in terms of repairs and what is a fair offer given the market conditions. Don't let your buyers go into contract then make unreasonable requests that everyone sees as an attempt to re-negotiate after the negotiating is done. Don't try to paint the seller in a corner with additional demands or credits right before the home is about to close. Be fair and negotiate fairly throughout the entire process.

One of my worst clients ever demanded an additional $10,000 at the very end of escrow from the seller or he would not close. I had already asked multiple times and the seller had refused. But the buyer knew the seller was in a hardship and was divorcing. He was playing dirty and nasty. Sadly, we were caught between a rock and a hard place, and we all had to give in to his outrageous demands.

Pre-pave your offer by letting the seller's agent know how strong and prepared your buyer is. Send the agent your buyer's letter to the homeowner that mentions specific things your buyer loves about the house. We actually have the buyers do a BombBomb video to the seller that says, "Hi, we love your house." This gives the sellers a personal connection with our buyers. It works really well because it puts a face to the offer on that piece of paper. Many sellers are only concerned with money, but others also really want their home to go to a good buyer. They want to leave their neighbors with a good neighbor. You never know what kind of seller you're going to get, so you should pull out every tool.

If there is a loan, have the lender call the seller's agent directly to explain how qualified your buyers are, how quickly the loan will take place, and even how long this lender has been in the business to show they can deliver. Submit the best offer possible to get the home your buyers want while still protecting their interests.

As negotiations continue, make sure your buyers understand the true cost to them of each part of the give and take. For example, explain what it might mean to them in the future if they overpay for the house today, or discuss whether they should argue about paying for the home inspection and risk losing the house.

Keep It Smooth After Acceptance: As we all know, so much happens between offer acceptance and close of escrow. Make sure your buyer understands this piece and what is expected of them. What information do they need to remove each contingency? When do they pay for the costs they've agreed to cover? For example, where I live, HOA inspections must be paid for before escrow (by the seller) and if you pay for the home inspection and the other inspections early, they usually give you a discount. The appraisal needs to be paid when it is ordered and prior to closing. Let the buyer know what they are responsible for paying and when it needs to be paid so they allocate the money and have it available.

When inspection reports come in, we sit down and go over them with the buyer and point out any red flags. We send them reminders of each deadline and the responsibilities on their end.

During this period, it is imperative that your buyers avoid any major purchases that might affect their credit or cash on hand, and that they do not have any late payments. They shouldn't buy any furniture on credit or take money out of bank accounts. Once they are in escrow, they need to tell you and the lender before they make any financial moves at all. If your buyer is getting cash from someone for the down payment and costs, this needs to be documented so it can be tracked and traced.

You also need to manage their expectations of time frames. Explain the difference between funding and recording. How does funding on a Friday affect their payments? In California, signing documents doesn't mean you take occupancy right away. The property has to be recorded which can take a few days—more if you run into holidays. Let them know when to schedule for utilities to be turned on or put in their name. We send our buyers the phone numbers they'll need, with a note, "Hey your house is closing in four days. Make sure you call and have the utilities transferred into your name the day your house closes. Here are all the phone numbers." We give this list to both seller and buyer so they can close out and begin utilities with no hassle.

A Few More Thoughts on Going Above and Beyond

Sometimes going above and beyond is about *not* doing something. Here are a few of those things to consider.

Do Them a Favor and Don't Take the Business

Another way you can go above and beyond for clients is to not take their business. If you live three hours away from a listing, no matter how sharp you are, realistically you can't do the job they deserve. You don't know the area and you don't know the market. You don't know what's great about their neighborhood. You won't want to spend the time driving back and forth to stay in touch with them and dealing with the house. Give these clients what they deserve by researching a terrific agent in their area and refer them to that agent. That local agent will go above and beyond to earn future referrals from you, and those clients will remember you as ethical and caring.

And do not call yourself an expert if you aren't one. If you haven't been educating yourself and keeping up with the market, don't pretend that you have. If you don't have expertise in a specific type of property, refer it to someone who does, or partner with someone who does, so you can learn.

If you can't put 100% effort in for your client for some reason, don't take their business. Maybe you're having personal challenges or you just can't relate to them or their property. Don't take the business if you can't give it your all. And, if you're a part time agent just playing around in the business, don't take the business. It sounds harsh, but selling or buying a home is one of the biggest investments anyone can make. You might be able to close the deal, but can you honestly say that you were the best person for the job and got the best result for that client? If you were in that client's position, wouldn't you want the most dedicated, professional agent you could get to handle your purchase or sale? There's too much at stake to accept business just for the paycheck.

About Dual Agency

A question our industry has debated for decades: Can you really serve your clients' best interests acting as a dual agent? It's a tricky area, but let me share how I handle it.

I recently listed a property that was a gorgeous single story on the golf course with a pool and RV access. It was one of the nicest homes in the neighborhood of Deer Ridge where I live. I knew we would get multiple offers even though the asking price was very high. And I happened to be working with a buyer who was interested in the house.

I took in all five offers, including my buyer's offer and an offer from an agent in my office, and presented them to my seller. Next, I got back to all the buyers' agents and told them to present their highest and best offers. I explained to the agents, and my seller and buyer that I would *not* look at these next offers so everyone would be on a level playing field.

Then I got together again with my buyer and we crafted our own highest and best offer. I told her that she probably needed to be in the range of $730,000 with terms that favored the seller to get the house. She took my advice and she got the house because we offered the highest price at the best terms, *fairly.*

At the end of the day, my seller got a great price and great terms. My buyer got the house she wanted. And I knew I had served both clients based on my knowledge and expertise, not because I used inside information unfairly.

Most agents don't know of a relatively new law in California that is only a few years old. If you write an offer, you can also submit a form CNE (Confidentiality Notice Disclosure) that is a confidentiality notice with your offer. It stipulates that the listing agent can't tell anybody else about that offer, including their own buyers or other agents. In other words, they can't use that information against you. I insist that all of my buyers' agents submit this form with every offer. I've used this form for over three years now. Still, every time we submit it, the other listing agent calls me and says, "What is this? I've never seen it before." It's an incredibly effective way to protect our clients, but few agents have taken the time to find out about it. Why? They have not researched and read about new forms as they come out. They are doing themselves and their clients a disservice. In fact, I was recently on a panel of real estate experts and not *one* of them knew what the CNE is!

In any form of dual agency, whether you have both buyer and seller or someone in your office has the buyer and you have the seller, you need to create a type of "firewall." Being loose with dual agency has gotten more than one broker sued.

Take the Next Step

1. Jot down 3 ideas you learned from this chapter. What can you implement in your current business? Do it!

2. So much of being a Community Market Leader has to do with educating people. Who are the great educators you know? What makes them good? How can you apply that to your business?

Be sure to visit **www.sell100homesbook.com** for free resources that will help you grow and automate your real estate business.

CHAPTER FIVE

Keep Yourself Growing

The reason I love continually learning is that I know there's a better, more effective way to do almost anything—even if you're already good at that thing. That's why I dive into situations that might stretch my thinking and challenge how I do things. Learning even one small thing each day allows me to keep expanding into the next "better way." Just as important, I implement that better way and continue to improve on it.

I wrote the statement above in the Introduction. I mentioned that if you want to become a Community Market Leader, you'll need to stretch and grow. You'll need to step out of your very comfy comfort zone and do things you've never tried before. And here's the deal: Even after you look around and see that you're now dominating your market, your presence is everywhere and clients are flocking to your door, you *still* need to keep growing. A Community Market Leader is more like a verb than a noun. It's not a place you get to where you can sit back, settle in and take a nap. Community Market Leader is a state of mind that has you continually improving, innovating, learning, and expanding in your mastery. And, if you ever get tired of real estate, you can apply that mindset to the next great thing you decide to do.

Growth is scary, but it's also exhilarating. And, more often than not, the thing that is scariest to you is the thing that will propel you to a new level. Controlled growth is the focus. This means growing and expanding after we've mastered the previous growth. You implement one new tool and become an expert in it prior to implementing new growth tools.

One of the scariest things I've ever done in real estate is to create my videos. I am not a natural public speaker. In fact, I *hate* public speaking. I get anxious and have actual panic attacks. In the old days when I did broker tours, I'd stand in front of twenty people I knew, and my palms would sweat and I'd be so nervous that I could hardly remember what I was supposed to say.

The idea of being in front of a camera to make a video that literally thousands of people might see was terrifying to me. Then, I figured out how valuable videos can be. Was I great when I started doing it? Nope. I had no idea what I was doing and I was so nervous that I spoke even faster than I normally do, kind of like those disclaimers at the end of prescription drug ads on T.V.

But I learned, and got better and better. And I felt excited and proud of myself each time I saw myself getting better. It helped me in all areas of my life and I stopped worrying so much that people were judging me or that I might make a mistake. No one else in real estate was taking that big leap and making videos. Even when I wasn't that great at it, I made an impact and stood out from the crowd. When I look back at my old videos, I can honestly say that they were horrible. Now they're much better. One video used to take me an hour. Now I can do one in literally five minutes.

Let me repeat myself: If an agent asked me what is the one single thing they can do to have the biggest and fastest impact on their business, I would tell them to start creating educational videos. The public doesn't know you from Adam and it's time to let them get to know you. You want them to see who and what you are all about. The more videos you distribute, the more you'll be remembered and perceived as the expert. Most people feel that all agents are all the same so they don't think it makes any difference whether they use you, their neighbor who's a Realtor®, or their co-worker's brother's wife.

It's your responsibility to show them that you are very different. When you expose the community to how different and knowledgeable you are, you start being seen as a person of authority. Today, I cannot go anywhere, and I mean *anywhere*, without someone telling me how much they love my videos. It might sound crazy, but my videos have definitely been the most impactful of just about anything I've done.

A video tells so much about who you are and how you run your business. You can show off without actually saying, "Hey, look how great I am!" You simply educate them about your process, the who's, what's, and why's of every aspect of your business. Through your videos, you can show that not all agents are the same and that it does make a difference whether they choose you or their Aunt Sally.

To get to where you want to be, you may have to do things you're afraid of doing. But look at the alternative: Most traditional agents spend their careers being constantly afraid of where their next lead is coming from. They're scared that their business isn't going to sustain itself. They're hamsters running on that wheel, operating basically out of fear about whether they'll able to make enough money to cover their own bills and whether they'll be able to close the next deal or land the next listing.

Personally, I'd rather face the fears of growing better and getting stronger, so I never again have those kinds of worries. I know that my pipeline will always be as full as I want it to be, and that I have the skill to make sure that 99% of my deals close and that I land around 93% of my listing appointments. I know that my business is sustainable no matter what the economy or our market is doing because I'm always adapting and changing. Right now, video is working magnificently but that doesn't mean it always will. I'm constantly adding and changing what and how I do videos so they continue to stand out.

For example, when I first started my videos were about three minutes. Now I've learned that shorter videos, around thirty seconds, are much more effective. I'm still learning and striving to be better. Had I not kept in touch with research and change, I wouldn't know this.

Most of us have reasons for not facing our fears. If I don't have a reason to cross over a river full of crocodiles then, heck no! I'm not doing it. But, if one of my daughters were in danger, or the thing I most wanted in the world was on the other side? You bet I'll cross it. In fact, I'd run right through those crocs to save my daughters or a loved one! The most important question you can ask yourself is, "Why do I want this?" Why are you reading this book? Why do you want to do more business? What will more consistent and greater income bring you? What would that look like for you personally, spiritually, within your family, and within yourself?

Why Do You Want This?

I'm not really fearful anymore but I certainly was when I first started this career. I left my teaching profession and dove into real estate full time, and I was scared to death. I had spent years learning to be a teacher and getting my Master's degree. But I just stopped full-boogie and jumped straight into real estate with very little training. I had the same fear many new agents have of, "Oh, my God, how am I going to pull this off?" And, as I mentioned before, this was at a time when my life had been turned upside down. I was in panic mode. But I made the decision, "Okay, Krista, you'll just have to stand out and be different, and learn how to be better than everyone else. You need to march in there and *just do it*, because failure is not an option."

I didn't have to discover my "why" at that point because it was staring me in the face. I had to support myself and my two little girls. Giving up or just skating by was not an option for me. Any time it got rough in the business, I just had to think about feeding my girls and making sure they had a roof over their heads. That motivation got me through all kinds of difficult times and inspired me to keep finding ways to better myself and my business.

Finding out your "why" is probably the most important key to your success in anything. Why do you want to be a Community Market Leader? Yes, it will bring you more money/clients/recognition. But why do you want these things? Your "why" is what is going to drive you. Your "why" is the force that keeps you going when you want to quit.

As I'm writing this book, I'm also developing my training materials, creating the brand for my training and coaching business, running my super successful real estate business and managing my "Teens Lifting Lives" non-profit program. My husband says, "You need to stop and take more time off." I tell him I can't stop. I need to push right now so that eventually *all* I'm doing is my coaching and training. That's my true passion and love. That's my "why."

My "why" is very specific. I am on a path of changing my professional career completely. I'm a very successful Realtor® and I love it. My personal "why" and what I am passionate about is teaching and making a positive impact on people. I want to empower people. I love inspiring people. I want to make people, like you, empowered in this business so you can lead the kind of life I'm living right now. I want to help other people enjoy prosperity, have more free time, and really enjoy what they're doing and feel good about it.

My daily affirmations include a bunch of statements that support this: "I positively affect every life I touch." "I am the number one real estate trainer in the world." "I love public speaking." "I speak slowly and my words are impactful." "I make a difference." "I am a Go-Giver."

I have several others, but you get the gist. Sometimes, at first, we need to fake ourselves out until we actually do believe in our dreams.

As much as I love real estate, I'm ready for something new. I'm ready for a new challenge. I've mastered my real estate business and I'm absolutely an expert at it. I'm ready to master something new. And I'm eager to help other people master what I've already mastered. Through my expertise and hard work, I've risen to the top and I know I can help other agents become leaders in their profession, year after year.

I also want more time with my husband and children. I want to be more present with them when we are engaging in conversations. I no longer want them to tell me "Mom, you're not listening to me" and walk away. I don't want to have to be chained to my phone all the time. I'm really crazy about wanting to respond to my clients and answer their questions quickly. Yet I'm at a point in my life where I'm ready to not have that stress. That's my "why" for working so many hours on my current business, as well as diving deep into my training and coaching. I want more time, the ability to let my clients know when I'll be working and when I won't. I don't want to be tied to my phone 24/7, never really feeling like I'm on vacation even when I am. I am working like a dog right now so eventually I will be able to work less and focus on my family and my non-profit.

Why is becoming a Community Market Leader important to you? What is going on in your life that you want to be different? What is your passion and how will stepping up your game in real estate support that?

One of my favorite teachers, Tony Robbins, says, *"People are not lazy. They simply have impotent goals - that is, goals that do not inspire them."* It's your inspirational "why" that will get you across that crocodile-infested river or get you in front of a video camera. It's your powerful dream, or the thing you love, that will help you face your biggest fears, encourage you to change the "safe" ways you've always done things, and keep you going as you're learning and feeling out of your comfort zone.

What is your "why?" Do you want to make more money? And, if you do, *why* do you want to make more money? Do you want more time? More time for what? Do you crave financial freedom? Do you want to pay off your house and become debt free? Do you need to have less anxiety? Write down all of your "why's."

Please do me a favor and don't skip this. Your "whys" are what make you do and act on what you need to in order to get the outcome that you want.

Who Do You Need to Be for the Business You Want?

I love this other quote from Tony Robbins:

> *"Beliefs have the power to create, and the power to destroy. Human beings have the awesome ability to take any experience of their lives, and create a meaning that disempowers them, or one that can literally save their lives."*

To become the Community Market Leader you want to be, you'll need to get rid of any limiting beliefs or doubts you might have. If you have any limiting beliefs, take them out of your head. If any type of negative thought comes in, change it around, and know that you deserve this, that you can do this, that this is attainable. In my "Teens Lifting Lives" group, one of the girls, Samantha, posted this on Facebook: "As Krista constantly drills into our heads to take the negative beliefs out and put the positive in, the more I do this the easier it becomes."

What I've taught you in this book is absolutely attainable. No one else is doing it in your area. You'll be the one to do it before anyone else does, and you're going to be successful at it. I need you to know that you're worthy and deserving of greatness. You deserve this.

Early on, I watched a webinar called Stealth Seminar. It's not real estate related, but I was learning how to do webinars and I wasn't completely comfortable making videos. I was already creating educational videos for people, and training buyers and sellers through webinars. But I knew I had a lot to learn. The guy teaching the class was so dorky, so frumpy. My first impression was "I can't believe this guy is on video." But after twenty seconds of watching him, I loved him. He was super smart, he was funny, and he definitely knew what he was talking about. I liked him even more because he was on camera being himself—frumpy and dorky and nerdy.

In fact, in one of his first videos, he was picking his nose and scratching his butt as he was getting ready to do a training and the camera was on him. I don't know if he did that on purpose or not, but it was hysterical. He didn't care that people were watching. He was just very real.

We're all unique in our own way, and you don't want to change to become just like me or just like anyone. As you change and grow, **you want to become *more* like yourself, not less**. To get the results of a Community Market Leader, you need to do the things a Community Market Leader does—but in your own unique way.

I was raised in a very religious family, and I rebelled against that religion growing up. I was super close to my family, but I ended up getting into trouble, going to juvenile hall, and I landed in a foster home. I had extremely low self-esteem. I always felt that nobody liked me and I always worried about what everybody thought of me. I didn't have a lot of self-confidence.

I've read a ton of self-help books. I've gone to massive counseling to help build up my self-esteem. I come across as a powerhouse woman in real estate because I know what I'm doing. But I still fight my basic insecurity every day. That's why I continue to read self-help books, constantly discovering ways to gain more confidence. I learned that the more I believe in myself, the more I love myself, and the more positive thoughts I have, the better I am for myself and others. The second a negative thought comes in, I take it out. I literally say to myself, "That's not true," then I say something positive.

When I started in this business, I thought I had to be someone different. I thought that people weren't going to like me; that I talked too fast, that I was too hyper, and that no one was going to take me seriously. I thought I needed to come across serious and calm. (If you know me, you know how impossible that is. I wake up with more energy than the Energizer Bunny!) You know what? Throughout the years, I've found the complete opposite. People love the fact that I have a lot of energy and talk fast. But my mind didn't believe this was true at first. I kept telling myself I needed to be more like this person or that person. That I wasn't enough as I am. It took me a while to understand that this line of thinking was just a self-imposed obstacle. I didn't need to be someone else. I needed to believe in myself and see that people like me for who I am.

I also had to realize that if people don't like the fun, crazy Krista, then they aren't the people I'm trying to attract into my life. Yet, as confident as I've become, there is still the little inner voice that screams, "You're not good enough." I fight it daily and pay special attention to my thoughts. For years, people have been asking me to teach and train. They made comments like, "I wish I had your enthusiasm and drive. If you ever become a coach, I'd love for you to take me on." I never believed them.

Recently, I have been reading many books that tell you to listen to those subtle hints, take hold of them, grasp them, and go for it. That's probably one of the reasons you're reading this book. I had to learn to listen to the Universe that was pointing me in the direction of my calling: To be of service and add value to all that I can.

I didn't need to become someone else. I just needed to become a better version of me in some areas and stop thinking negatively. The second I stop believing in myself, whatever I'm going after is never going to happen.

Today, I know there's nothing I can't achieve that I put my mind to. I know I need to work hard for my goals. They won't come for free and will not always be easy to achieve. I know I need to keep learning and implement what I learn until I've mastered it. But, as long as I keep applying myself and believing in myself, I know I can achieve just about anything. I remind myself of this frequently and you'll need to do the same.

We're so used to negative thoughts that we hardly recognize them. A common negative thought in real estate is that if someone already dominates an area, you'll never catch up no matter what you do. That's 110% inaccurate. All you have to do is stand out and show your extraordinary value, and you can outshine that person over time. This won't happen overnight or even within a couple of months. But, once the momentum builds for you, especially using the power of social media and the internet, your business will take off. However, if you don't believe it will or you truly believe that you can't do this, you might as well throw in the towel now. I just love this saying from Henry Ford: ***"Whether you think you can, or you think you can't–you're right."*** I just love that! Think you can because you can. It might feel easier to fall prey to your self-limiting beliefs. But the thoughts that say, "I can" and "I am" something positive are the ones that will propel you forward.

Other negative statements I hear a lot are, "I can never learn the technology. I'm too old to learn the technology. I'm not good with computers." That's BS. I suck at computers. I'm not at good at technology at all, but I studied and I learned. Everything I do for my marketing, I learned by taking trainings and watching webinars. Using YouTube, you can learn to do almost anything. It was different ten years ago, but today you can find thousands of classes online to learn the technology you need. You just have to put the time and investment into learning. I am still constantly learning to be innovative, and learning how I can use technology to stand out, be more efficient, and make a positive impact on my clients.

Certain programs and apps are easier than others. Figure out what the easier ones are and start there. Take it step by step, learning one app and implementing it into your business then learning another one. (In my Community Market Leader course, I teach every aspect of the technology you need for this business.) I continue to add and implement as time changes because technology and innovations change. It's a constant!

Another limiting belief I've heard from coaching clients: "I don't have the time to do all of the things you're saying to do." My response is always, **"If you really want to have more time, if you really want to have more freedom, you'll make the time."** We can all make time for things that are important to us, right? By making a few adjustments in your life, like waking up an hour earlier and skipping your favorite TV shows, you'll find plenty of time to do those things that will give you so much more reward. "Limited time" is just another of those limiting beliefs, not the truth.

Think about this: Once you take the time to do things differently and learn to generate leads and clients more efficiently, you'll be thrilled you took the time to learn and implement new technologies. It's much better than sitting at an open house for four hours or taking up half of your Saturday, walking doors or making cold calls. I don't know about you, but I'd much prefer going on a hike with my family or hitting up the Farmers' Market on Saturday.

My mind is not all gung-ho or in Pollyanna mode every day and every minute of the day. Like everybody, I have negative thoughts pop up. I've learned to take note that I'm having that negative thought or doubt, then I say something opposite. I'll say things like, "You're likable, you're enthusiastic, you speak clearly, you talk slowly, and you are totally calm (okay, this last one will never happen, but I can dream!)." And I'll say it with feeling, like I'm my own cheering squad, and drown out the noise of the negative stuff in my head. For help with this, I'd recommend reading books like: *I'm a Badass* by Jen Sincero, *The 10X Rule* by Grant Cardone, *The Thank You Economy* by Gary Vaynerchuk, *Mindset: The New Psychology of Success* by Carol Dweck, *The Five Second Rule* by Mel Robbins, and *How to Win Friends and Influence People* by Dale Carnegie, *Expert Secrets* by Russell Brunson.

Business Coaches and Mentors

> *"Real experts seek out constructive, even painful feedback. They're also skilled at understanding when and if a coach's advice doesn't work for them."*

—Harvard Business Review July-August 2007

You don't have to create your success from scratch. Don't reinvent the world. Follow in the footsteps of someone who has the success you want. When people achieve great success, typically they've had a role model. They've emulated somebody who is already successful, studied what they did then copied those things. **You're in luck—you have me!** You can copy exactly what I've done to close 100 to 169 units per year for the past sixteen years whether the market was up, down or sideways. Taking the information in this book and *applying* it is the key to getting there, along with continuing to change and adapt.

I've invested a lot of time and energy into educating myself about real estate and business in general. Recently, I've also focused on personal improvement to step more fully into my coaching and training business. I'm working with a couple of business coaches to help me structure my coaching and training business. I'm taking an NLP (Neuro Linguistic Programming) course to help me release more of my fears and limiting beliefs and teach others how to do this. I'm learning so many new things and stretching myself. I feel so inspired by this that I can hardly sleep at night.

As I'm focusing on a whole new business of training, and coaching, I'm still running my real estate business, selling around 150 houses per year with a goal to continue to increase that in the upcoming years. I have plenty of energy to do all of this because I'm so excited about it. It's exciting to learn! Implement what you've learned and start seeing the results. As you continue to grow, you'll see how it really works. As you step into this process and implement then master what I'm showing you, you'll feel that excitement, energy, and enthusiasm as well. You have the secret weapon: You have YOU! You'll have to do a lot more than just desire something. You'll need to implement and continue to do so.

First let's talk about mentors. I have mentors both in and outside of real estate, people I really want to emulate. There are certain people you want to emulate and others that you really should *not* emulate. Choose carefully. Make sure the people you emulate really have the type of success you want, those who will sincerely show you all you need to know and are authentically the kind of person you want to be. Ask a few questions in considering a mentor:

Do they really have the success you want? Several people out there teach courses in how to do the real estate business, but they haven't really achieved success in the industry themselves. They are more interested in succeeding by *teaching* success than succeeding in the business. Others, often the person your broker first hooks you up with, have been in the business for decades. They still do things the way they did thirty years ago, or quite frankly even five year ago. They may still be productive because they've built a strong client base over the years. But they don't know how to build a business in today's market and they certainly don't know what it takes to become a Community Market Leader. Make sure the people you're learning from have actually done what they're teaching you to do. Even better, are currently doing it and doing it well.

You don't want to emulate the person who's doing just enough to get by until they're ready to retire. You certainly don't want to copy their habits if they're wandering into the office around 10:00 AM, chit-chatting on the phone for a few hours and doing the bare minimum for their clients. You don't want to emulate someone who is doing the business the way everyone else is doing it.

Instead, look for the person who stands out from the crowd. Emulate the person who is clearly professional at what they do and who is still passionate about real estate and their clients. Model yourself after the person who is excited to learn new things and try different approaches. Imitate the agent who knows the business inside and out, who admits when he doesn't know an answer then finds the answer. Choose the person who takes pride in the quality of everything they do, who treats every listing like a million-dollar listing and every client like their new best friend.

My title rep visits me often and personally brings me my commission checks. It's important for her to continue to develop a relationship with me. She is always telling me, "Krista everyone is always asking me what it is that you do to get all the business." She finally learned to say, "What isn't she doing?" Quite frankly, that's the truth. Find someone like that. Not just a fly-by-night agent who had a good year or two, but someone who consistently stays on top through any up or down market.

Are they sincerely offering what you need to know? In real estate, our first "mentor" is often a senior agent who just wants an assistant or a gofer. They'll teach you how to fill out forms and maybe what to say on a cold call. But mainly they're interested in someone who is willing to spend weekends holding their listings open for them. They want someone to do the legwork they're not interested in. I ran into this myself. After my first year, I was very flattered when a top agent in the area asked me to partner with her. As I worked with her, I realized that she just wanted someone she could rely on to do all the work because she was planning to move. What I thought was a potential mentor turned out to be someone who took advantage of me.

Sometimes senior agents want to help, but they're afraid of giving up "the secret sauce." They have some tricks up their sleeves that could really help you out, but they're afraid to share it. Make sure the person you choose as a mentor is generous with what they know. In fact, learn from someone who isn't in your area at all. Go onto Zillow or research top agents around the country. See what they are doing, implement it, and do what they do *better*. If it's working for them, it can work for you. Don't ever stop, keep growing!

Are they the kind of person you want to be? Maybe you have a hot shot agent in your office who is willing to mentor you along but you sense that he isn't quite ethical in how he operates. Don't even go near him. His reputation—which *will* get out no matter how clever he thinks he is—will taint you, as well.

Or maybe the best Realtor® around is a workaholic with no time for herself, her family, or her community. Working hard is one thing, but is that who you want to be? Most of us want success for the quality of life it can bring, not just to build up more money in our bank accounts than we could ever use.

I mentioned Tony Robbins earlier. I've been to many of his events and read his books. I look at him and see his compassion, empathy, and drive to help everybody. He's amazing at what he does. He's innovative in his thoughts and techniques, and he just goes for it. He is knowledgeable about so many things, from how to make and keep your money to personal self-help. He goes above and beyond with everything he does in his life, from giving back, to supporting charities, to feeding the homeless. He's a total giver. In fact, my affirmation is, "I want to be the Tony Robbins of real estate. I want to help as many people succeed as I can. I will positively affect every life I touch. The more I give, the more I get. I positively attract anything and everything I need into my business to be a complete success."

I sat in one of his four-day training events with my husband and my fifteen-year-old and eighteen-year-old daughters. Each day was anywhere from twelve to eighteen hours, and we were totally engaged and energized the entire time. This guy has apparently made around 440 million dollars, yet when he's up there you can tell he's sincere about wanting to help people, wanting to change lives, and wanting to do things for the right reasons.

There were over ten thousand people at that particular event and he gave us each a book. It's called *Money: Master the Game*, and I'd encourage everyone to read it. This book isn't just some throw-away that you can read in two hours. It has a lot of valuable content that you can apply. When I thought about writing this book, my goal was to give that same kind of value.

I am using coaches like Suzanne Evans, Russell Brunson, and Tony Robbins Coaching to help me structure my business, improve my public speaking skills, and work on personal growth and development. I started working with each of them because they resonate so well with me. Suzanne and Russell have helped me set boundaries with my clients, and have worked with me on how I speak to people and the language I use. Another business coach, is teaching me how to tell a story on stage, and how to speak clearly and have confidence when I'm on stage. The Tony Robbins Coaching Program is helping me both personally as well as with time management in my business. I'm working with a business coach to learn how to build a business that gives you a lifestyle of freedom in two years or less. I'm also studying a program called Cash Flow that teaches you how to "sell without selling."

I met one coach at seminar where someone else was the primary speaker. She gave a 20-minute presentation and I was totally impressed. She got up on stage and spoke clearly, effectively, and with authority. I felt like she was talking directly to me. I didn't even have to think about it. I immediately signed up for her course. She resonated more with me in her 20-minute presentation than the person who put on the event and who spoke for the majority of the three days. She showed up like a leader. She is a powerhouse, knows her stuff, and is confident. That is how I come across in my business.

When you know you do a great job, you feel confident and command authority and respect.

That is how you want to feel about a mentor or coach. That you resonate with not only what they teach but who they are.

Constant Education

We talked about education to increase your expertise in the industry and to stay current with market trends and the economy. But, to succeed as a Community Market Leader, you need to go beyond that. You need to step out of your industry and focus on getting better at a number of things. Maybe you need to become a better public speaker. Maybe you need to increase your confidence. Maybe you need to learn to handle your finances more intelligently or responsibly. **We all have areas that need improving.**

I've done so much work over the past sixteen years in real estate that I feel like I left my own personal growth and development behind. Over the past year or so, I've started focusing on that area. My goal is to enhance my speaking skills and become better with my general selling skills through better listening. (For example, someone might say, "I can't afford to sell," or "Your commission is too high," but what they're really saying is, "I don't see the value in what you're giving me yet.")

Find those areas where you can improve and make a plan. Stay in a learning mode *always* so that expanding your knowledge is a consistent theme in your life. Challenge yourself to become better at something every single week.

Educating yourself and getting new credentials will help you within your business. I cannot tell you how many people called me because of all the credentials I have after my name. They always chuckle while telling me that. I just respond, "I take my business very seriously. I owe it to the clients I serve to give as much value as possible and I can only do so through continuous education."

(I've listed my credentials and why I think they are important in the Resources section.)

Staying Energized

To become and continue to be a Community Market Leader takes a lot of energy. Rather than taking the minimum requirement of continuing education, Community Market Leaders are educating themselves on a weekly basis, and implementing what they're learning. Community Market Leaders aren't content with their last good idea, they're constantly improving month after month on what they're producing. They ask, "How can I make this better for my clients and the community I serve? How can I give even more value?" They constantly test to find out what's working and what's not. Their business is constantly evolving based upon new technologies and innovations. And, because they're doing all of that, their business is growing exponentially.

It takes a lot of energy and energy comes from enthusiasm.

I want you to be enthusiastic about becoming a Community Market Leader, not just going along for the ride. I want you to be enthusiastic as you're learning, and enthusiastic when you're implementing. Be enthusiastic when something doesn't work because it's teaching you what does. Be enthusiastic about even the smallest of gains. If you're not usually an enthusiastic kind of person, work on that. It will bring you amazing rewards.

I don't wake up happy every single day. When I was going through my divorce, I was so sad, lonely, angry and panicked. I'll never forget one morning on the first Thanksgiving that my daughters were at their dad's (my ex-husband's). The house was empty and quiet. I just sat in the kitchen alone and crying. Just weeks prior my family had been ripped apart and I felt like there was no hope. I missed them so much my heart hurt. I felt very sorry for myself. It was tough, but I still tried my hardest to be as positive as I could, and show up with enthusiasm. I put a happy face on, and I continue to do that every day.

I still have rough days, but it's how I choose to approach these days that counts. It's how I show up. I'm an Audible nut, I love listening to books all the time. I go back and forth between them. This morning I was listening to *How To Master the Art of Selling* by Tom Hopkins. He says that as sales people we will always have challenges. We need to welcome challenges and should be grateful for them because that means it offers an obstacle to overcome. He reminds us that in sales we are going to hear "no" more than once. We are going to see a listing we thought for sure was going to be ours go to another agent. If it hasn't happened to you yet, it will. Buck up. Sales can be hard. Just learn and grow from the challenges and move on. There is no power at all in regret, shame or guilt. Just ask if you could have done anything differently or better, and do that next time. Not everyone is going to connect with you and that's okay. We can't win them all!

You have to show that you love what you're doing. Being enthusiastic is basically being in love with people, being in love with your job, being in love with serving your clients. That's enthusiasm. I love what I do and I love people. Clients can hear that in my voice and in how I speak with them. I am not just in it for the money. Yes, I make excellent money, but money comes because I place people before things, always. The money then always follows. And please, love what you do. My quote for business is, "When You Do What You Love, People Love What You Do!"

Take the Next Step

1. *Figuring out your "why" is one of the most important things you can do to become successful. Set aside at least 30 minutes of quiet time to answer these questions: Why is becoming a Community Market Leader important to you? What's going on in your life that you want to be different? What is your passion and how will stepping up your game in real estate support that passion?*

Be sure to visit **www.sell100homesbook.com** for free resources that will help you grow and automate your real estate business.

CHAPTER SIX

Setting Goals and Your Action Plan

If you're a person who aims high in life and I've done my job in writing this book, you're probably eager to get started on the path to become a Community Market Leader and reap all the benefits that go with it. Good for you! You've spent time in the last chapter thinking about your *"why."* Now let's put together a plan to get you where you want to go. To start, it's important to understand how to set effective goals so when the going gets a little tough—which it will—you have the juice to keep going to achieve what you're after. It takes work to get what you want, but you can do anything you put your mind to.

I've always been the kind of person who decides what she wants and goes for it. I was setting goals long before I really knew how to do it. My goals—and my determination to achieve them—have helped me create an incredible business and a really satisfying personal life. I'd like the same for you. I've studied a lot of different goal-setting systems and taken what I think is the best from each. If your goals have produced mediocre results so far, it might be due to the specific *way* you're setting goals.

Start with Your Vision, Your Aim

In working with goals, you have to begin with the big picture before you narrow it down into smaller goals and tasks. This is on the level of "What inspires me?" It's very similar to your "why," but it's fleshed out in Technicolor. It's that clear vision of what you ultimately want.

For example, I mentioned that one of my "why's" is to spend more quality time with my family. Here's what that looks like in vision form:

> *We have a blended family, but by looking at us you would never know it. My relationship with my stepson is stronger than ever, and he confides in me because he trusts me to keep what he says confidential. My daughters have so much confidence that when they walk into the room you can't help but notice. For all of us, our main mission in life is to be good and to help others succeed and become better. Our family makes it a priority to spend time together and we put each other first. Our entire family is full of abundance and gratitude and we take nothing for granted. All of this stems from the fact that my husband and I are so strongly connected.*

When I stop and visualize this, I get excited and happy. I can practically taste how sweet this is! It's not yet set up in "end goal" form (which I'll show you next), but it is definitely inspirational.

In his book, *Awaken the Giant Within: How to Take Immediate Control of Your Mental, Emotional, Physical, and Financial Destiny*, Tony Robbins outlines how he starts the process of setting goals. I like this process because you can do it in less than an hour and don't have to spend hours and hours sweating over goalsetting.

You begin by brainstorming, writing down possibilities very quickly so you don't censor yourself. In this first stage, don't get hung up on the details of *how* to make this happen, but let it flow and fill in details later. You need to make this first list fun and inspirational. Remember how you felt when you were a kid about the things you wanted to be or have? Your list of goals should make you feel excited like that.

Tony divides goals up into four categories: Personal Development, Career and Financial, Toys and Adventure, and Contribution goals. Personally, I prefer the categories of Marriage, Family, Business, Personal, and Giving Back. Divide your goals into any categories that make sense to you.

Within each of your categories, brainstorm a list of goals for five minutes. My list under Family looks something like this:

- *Kids all being close and getting along*
- *More connection with my stepson*
- *My daughters feel more self-confident*
- *Our family focuses on giving*
- *Spending quality time together*
- *Working together in my business*

When your list is complete, take one minute to give each goal a timeframe of 1 year, 2 years, or 3 years, and mark them as 1 (everything 1 year or less), 2, or 3. (Most of the items on my list above are within one year.) Next, choose one of your 1-year or less goals that is most important and write for two minutes about *why* it's so important to you. Done! Go to the next category and do the same process.

Using part of my vision above, I might write something like: *I want more connection with my stepson so he will confide in me because I know it's tough to be a teenager and I know I can help him. I want to provide him with the mother he never had and contribute to his life. I love him and I want him to feel that love. I want him to feel the certainty that, no matter what happens, I've got his back.*

What is your vision in each of your categories? I highly recommend you stop and do this 30-minute process and create your vision in at least one category before I show you how to create specific end goals.

Here's another personal example, my vision in the Business category:

> *My CML® coaching and training is very successful and growing exponentially. My Homes By Krista business is also thriving and both businesses are running like well-oiled machines. My husband and three children all work alongside me. Our mission is to encourage others and help them live more prosperous lives. Both businesses are recognized nationally within our industry. I totally enjoy speaking to large groups and am thrilled that I am making such a difference in the lives of others.*

That may not be your personal vision, but can't you see how a vision like that would get you leaping out of bed in the morning, eager to dive into your day? That's what you want for your own vision. Take a few minutes and go through the 30-minute process to jot down your vision and why you want it.

Putting Your Vision into End Goals

In his training sessions, Dr. Matthew James, CEO of The Empowerment Partnership who has taught Neuro Linguistic Programming (NLP) for about 30 years, emphasizes setting effective goals. He calls your vision "aim goals." An aim goal is the direction you want to go in life. It never really has an end point, but it inspires you to keep moving forward. Dr. James says that an "end goal" is different. It's a specific result you want and after you achieve it, you move on to another end goal. Your end goals are like stepping stones toward your vision. To set end goals, Dr. James uses the acronym "SMART" (like many other teachers). Where an aim goal (vision) can be broad, your end goal has to be SMART.

S: The S stand for *specific* and *simple.* If your end goal isn't specific, you don't have a clear target. For example, if you say, "I want to make lots of money," what does that even mean? Thirty thousand per year? Four million per year? When you put a specific number to it, you can picture that result and begin to figure out what to do to get there. So, you might write down, "I am making $10,000 a month by June 30, 20XX without having to work weekends and late nights."

Simple means that it is basic enough to explain to a 7-year-old. In his trainings, Dr. James explains that your unconscious mind (which is always at work to support you) needs very simple instructions. So, it's better to say, "I have a steady net income of $27,000 per month" rather than, "I want my portfolio to earn an average of 3.7% while I close 5 units per month, so my commissions total $22,500 and I pick up an additional $3,500 in referral fees." Too complicated! Keep it simple.

M: The M stands for *measurable* and *meaningful.* If you can't measure your end goal, how will you know when you've gotten there? Some goals are easier to measure than others. Take the example of my family goals: How will I know when my stepson and I are closer? I might set the end goal to be, "My stepson and I talk for five to ten minutes at least twice per week, and we go out to lunch alone at least once per month." That's something I can measure.

Meaningful means that the end goal has to be important to *you.* Sometimes we try to create goals based on what other people want for us or what we think we *should* do. Those goals won't inspire us. If your goal is to sell 10 units this quarter because your broker thinks you should, how exciting is that? But, if *you* decide you want to sell 10 units because you're determined to beat your own record, or because you want to pay off your debts so you can sleep at night, that goal will have some real juice behind it.

A: According to Dr. James, A stand for three things: *achievable, all areas of your life,* and *as if now. Achievable* means that on some level you believe you can achieve this goal. That's not to say that the goal should be easy. Easy goals aren't very exciting. Your goal should be a stretch and take some extra effort and focus on your part. But, if in your heart, you're convinced you can't hit your goal, you'll be fighting yourself the whole way. Take your "impossible" goal and just back off a notch. If you think selling 100 units is impossible for you this year, set your goal at 25. Then, when you hit that goal, ratchet your next goal up to 40 or 50.

All areas of your life means to take into consideration your life balance. For example, if you're setting a huge goal for your business this year, where will that additional time and energy come from? How can you make sure that you don't mess up your personal life, your health, and your sanity while pursuing your big goal? If you simply put blinders on and focus solely on one goal, you'll find that other areas will suffer—and when they do, you'll get thrown off course. You may have to get creative, but figure out ways to keep all areas of your life on track as you pursue your big goals.

As if now means that goals are always stated in the present. Rather than saying, "I *will* make $4M in 20XX," you keep it in present tense and say, "I *make* $4M in 20XX." There are a number of reasons for this. First, it keeps you accountable. When you say that you *will* do something, it is always out somewhere in the future. When someone else points out, "Hey, but you're *not* doing that," you always have the excuse of, "Yeah, but I *will* someday." When you state, "I *am* doing this," you can look yourself in the mirror and know if it's true or not. Also, Dr. James explains that if you use a future tense, your unconscious mind will keep pushing that goal out into the future rather than helping you achieve it now.

R: The R stands for *realistic* and *responsible*. Even though your goal is possible based on everything in your life right now, is it realistic? A lot of seemingly impossible things really are possible. The question is whether it's realistic to expect that end result for you at this time. Maybe you need more training, or to build a stronger foundation to reach your end goal. If so, those things should be set as your first goals.

Responsible has to do with what NLP calls "ecology." Is your goal good not only for you but also for the other people involved— your family, your community, and even our planet? If your goal does harm in any way, you'll run into a lot of resistance, not only from the outside but from within yourself as well.

T: The T is for *timed* and *toward what you want*. Your end goal has to have a specific timeframe so you'll know how much energy it will take to achieve it. For example, say you want to double your business. The goal, "I double the revenue from my business within three months from now" is a totally different animal than "I double the revenue from my business within the next three years." Use a specific date for your goal and calendar it so you can keep track of your progress.

Toward what you want means to set a positive goal, not a negative one. Negative goals are, "I am no longer 40 pounds overweight" or "I do not have to scramble every month to pay my bills." Research shows that when people have negative goals, they lose motivation as they get closer to the end result. So, when that person hits the point where he is only *10* pounds overweight or where she can cover *most* of her bills, they stop feeling as stressed so they slack off. With a positive goal, you're inspired to keep going until you feel the reward of the achievement. To turn them into positive goals, those negative goals could be rewritten as, "I weigh

180 pounds" or "I have an extra $1,000 in my account after paying off all my bills each month."

Personally, when I'm learning something new I find examples very helpful. Here are some examples of well-written end goals and others that are not.

GOOD: My CML® business nets over $6M by March 21, 20XX

NOT GOOD: My CML® business will take off and be highly successful sometime next spring.

GOOD: By May 15, 20XX, I have booked four 3-day CML® trainings and signed up 4,500 participants.

NOT GOOD: Next year, I will do several trainings in front of huge audiences for my CML® business.

GOOD: As of December 15, 20XX, I am working 3 hours per day at Homes by Krista and 5 hours per day at CML® coaching and training.

NOT GOOD: Before next year, I will work less on Homes by Krista and more on my coaching and training, while still getting more personal time.

GOOD: As of January 1st, 20XX, my husband and I dedicate one evening per week to each other, going out and doing something fun together.

NOT GOOD: By next year, my husband and I will be spending more quality time together.

Putting it All Together

Begin with your visions (or aim goals) then translate them into good end goals. I like to set short-term (within 3 months), mid-term (6 to 12 months), and long term (over a year) goals. Write your goals down. Even if you have no idea how to achieve a goal, write it down and think about it every day. Place your vision and end goals on your bathroom mirror, put them on your steering wheel, tape them to your laptop screen. Every time you see them, think about *why* you want those goals. Read them every morning when you wake up and every night before you go to sleep. I even read them aloud into my iPhone so I can listen to them as often as I can whenever I have a minute.

I also like to create vision boards. I use a poster board and find pictures that represent what I'm going after. I might have a family on a beach for a vacation I want, or a graph showing a business increasing its profits. Whenever I look at my visions boards, I remind myself of why I want those things and how great it will feel when I get there.

A friend of mine even used a vision board to lose weight. She had been on some medication that caused her to gain 30 pounds in a very short time. It freaked her out to see herself in the mirror. She gathered photos of herself at her normal weight and lots of pictures of slim bodies. She plastered them all over her mirror so that when she looked in the mirror, that's all she saw—not her overweight self. She says this vision "board" inspired her to do all the things she needed to do to become her prior size again.

Next, take action on your end goals. Every day take one step, big or small, that moves you closer to that goal. Having a dream without clearly written goals is just a fantasy. And **a goal without action behind it is just fiction.** Activities toward your goals should show up on your calendar. If they don't, your goal must not be very important to you, right?

The action steps you take toward your goals don't have to be huge, but they do need to be consistent. For example, you may have a goal to "Create a digital marketing platform by December 1, 20XX." You might start by researching various CRMs, then setting a deadline to choose one. You might review my videos, then set a date to create your own first three videos. The important thing is to do something that takes you one step closer to your goal every day.

Your Community Market Leader Start-Up Plan

Now that you have the process for setting goals, let's create a series of goals around becoming a Community Market Leader. This is important. Take the time to do it and please reach out to me once you do and tell me about your successes. I'm excited to see and hear about your growth.

First, write down your vision of what that will look like when you've achieved it. How do you feel? What in your life looks different professionally, personally, and within your family? What kind of business will you have? Who will be working with you? How will your days be spent? What kind of income will you bring in?

Next, spend a few minutes to write down *why* you want this. How does it make your life better? What would be exciting about it to you?

Now set up a number of end goals using the SMART acronym. I'd suggest you put them in these categories (you'll notice that some overlap):

Engaging the Community
Creating Educational Videos
Creating an Online Presence
Engaging Past Clients
Self-Education
Trends in the Economy, Real Estate
Technology
Personal Growth
Professional Skills
Best Practices in Business
Employing Technology
Setting Up CRM
Lead Generation and Tracking
Using Social Media for Marketing and Community Engagement
Enhancing Your Marketing
Revamping Current Marketing Materials

Designing Systematic Marketing Process
Creating Innovative Approaches
Developing Your Brand and Niche
Solidifying Your Business
Identifying Resources
Hiring an Assistant
Creating a Team
Systematizing All Processes, Start to Finish

Within each of these categories, figure out what you want to get accomplished in 30 days, 60 days, and 90 days. Write those things down as SMART end goals. What can you do alone and where do you need assistance? To get you started, here are some Action Challenges that will yield fast results, and that you can *easily* accomplish within the first 90 days:

Action Challenge #1: Create your first educational video: Choose a relevant topic that is getting a lot of buzz right now and create a 30-second video about it. Go to Inman News, real estate Facebook groups, or Google to find a good topic. Do not get stumped and don't over think it—just do it! Use your iPhone to record the video. When it's done, send it to Fiverr or another source to have it edited and annotations added. Then upload it on social media sites like Facebook, Instagram, and Twitter. Done!

Action Challenge #2: Gather client testimonials: Contact past clients to get testimonials to post online. Create an email and send it out, including links to Yelp, Zillow, Trulia, and Google. Send your first email out to at least forty clients using some kind of incentive (see example email below). Then send a similar email out to five other past clients every week. (It doesn't look good to get a ton of reviews one week then nothing for months, so stay consistent in this.) Put it on the calendar so you remember to do this consistently, rather than getting a bunch of testimonials all at one shot. Also, put it on your transaction check list to ask for testimonials after a closing.

Example:

> *Subject Line: Thank you so much for Everything!! I'd love to enter you into a drawing for $250.00 and I'm only sending this to a total of 40 people so the chances of winning are high.*
>
> *Dear [Name of Homeowner],*
>
> *I hope all is well with you :-)*
>
> *I was hoping that you could help me. I'm very much trying to enhance my on-line presence. The best way is actually through Zillow and Google+. YELP is also huge! Would you mind taking a few minutes to write a review for me? Zillow attracts about 90,000 viewers each month alone, just in your zip code. So, many people are looking and using these services to help find their agent. It will definitely help me increase my business. I know you are so incredibly busy so you'll be enrolled in a drawing for a $250.00 Amazon card.*
>
> *Here are the links to leave the reviews on Zillow, Trulia, Yelp, & Google+ (include links here)*
>
> *I appreciate your time and efforts. Thanks so very much.*
>
> *Your Real Estate Professional for LIFE*
>
> *Krista Mashore*

Obviously, you should write an email that sounds like you, not like me. Even better, create a *video* request for testimonials. Your email can have the same subject line and an individualized greeting, but the video can be made as a generic request. Send this out to a minimum of five people every week.

Action Challenge #3: Prep for Your Next Listing Appointment: Create an awesome property website of an existing listing or a home you have sold in the past. (If you don't have any listings of your own, ask a colleague if you can use one of their listings. You can even use your own home or a friend's—you are just creating an example of the type of marketing you will do for a client.) I recommend using Agent Marketing for your site because it has so many features and is user-friendly. Have a professional photographer and videographer takes shots of the home and edit them. Take screen shots of all the features of Agent Marketing: Neighborhood Demographics, Photos, Contact Me, Virtual Tour, What's Nearby. Upload these onto your iPad or make color copies for your listing presentation. You will use these to show prospective clients what the website you'll create for them can do.

Be sure to familiarize yourself with the Text Feature of Agent Marketing. It's very easy to use. One very effective thing to do on a listing presentation is to take out your phone, and have the seller take out their phone, then show them how it works. It's even more effective to show them that, when someone texts for information about a property, the system sends you (the agent) the phone number of the person inquiring so you can follow up instantly. I can demonstrate right then by having my clients send a text regarding one of my properties so they see the whole process.

Action Challenge #4: More Prep for Your Next Listing Appointment: Create a Property List Report to use during your listing presentation. Create an ad on Facebook that promotes one of your listings with information from List Reports. List Reports will show everything surrounding a specific property, such as schools and their scores, nearby restaurants (with ratings and pricing), local golf courses and parks, as well as pharmacies, grocery stores, and gyms. (If you don't have your own listings, ask a colleague if you can create an ad for one of theirs—it will be a win-win!) Upload this example ad on your iPad or take screenshots and print color copies of the ad to take to your next listing appointment to show prospective sellers what you can do for them.

Action Challenge #5: Generate Leads Online: Sign up for Home Evaluation software, then create a landing page (go online and research how to create landing pages) to attract homeowners who might be interested in selling. Hire My Out Desk, Fiverr, or any other resource to get you going on this. Look for eye-catching photos that stand out, and tell a story that reflects the market you're in and the homeowners you want to attract.

Be creative! Don't just title your page, "Find Out the Value of Your Home." Brainstorm innovative headlines for several different target markets. "Your Neighbor's House Just Sold for 6% MORE Than the Previous Home Sale—What's Your Home Worth Now?" or "Is This the Perfect Time to Downsize? Find Out What Your Home Could Sell For."

Create a target market ad for your landing page that will attract the people you want from the list you made. Post the ad on several social media platforms. Spend at least $20 on each ad (I spend $200 on mine). Schedule a new ad to run twice every month. Pay attention to which ads and which platforms get you the most response.

Action Challenge #6: Generate More Leads Online: The Home Evaluation software is a great tool to attract people and capture their contact information, but what else can you think of? The key is that it needs to be something that is truly *valuable* to people.

One program that has worked incredibly well for me is called The Local Heroes Program. I teamed up with a local lender and we offer discounts to teachers, fire fighters, police officers, and men and women in the military—basically anyone who serves the community. The lender researches programs offered by the federal government, cities, and state that are geared to help people in different forms of public service. In addition to the government programs, between the two of us, we offer special discounts:

1. $100 off a home inspection
2. Reimbursement on appraisals ($500+ dollar value)

3. Reimbursement of termite inspection ($250 value)

4. $1,000 towards closing costs

Our only disclaimer is: "If buyer fails to purchase for any reason, the buyer will incur the costs. Offer only valid for one home."

If you were in the military or on the police force, wouldn't you be attracted to that page?

Your action challenge is to come up with at least five ideas for landing pages that offer value to a certain segment of the market. Maybe it's first time buyers, or seniors looking to sell their home to move into assisted living. Maybe it's non-English speakers or investment buyers. What special value could you offer? Come up with your ideas and implement one per month by creating a landing page then posting an ad for it on social media (you'll reach far more people if you sponsor or pay for your ad). Not all of your ideas will be home runs. But the ones that are can be gold!

Action Challenge #7: Create Your First Market Trends Video: Choose a particular city or area you're interested in and study its current stats. Create a brief video that reviews those stats—active, pending, sold—and how current inventory affects buyers and sellers. Research what's in the pipeline and include any good market prognoses from reputable sources you come across.

Again, don't stress over this! Gather your information and think about what that information means to potential clients. Then just be conversational, as if you met someone at a party who asked you about the market. Once your video is complete, shoot it off to Fiverr for editing and adding annotations. Upload it on social media sites like Facebook, Instagram, and Twitter. Email it to your contact list and ask for feedback.

Action Challenge #8: Create Some "Keeping Connected" Videos: Brainstorm at least ten videos you can send out to various people (clients, past clients, cooperating agents, prospective clients, or anyone in your sphere of influence). For example, your video might say, "Thanks for listing your home with me" or "I hope you are happy in your new home." It could be a Happy Birthday or Happy Anniversary video, or a Get Well Soon video. Set aside fifteen minutes *every day* to send out five videos.

This may seem like a lot. But think of it as making five quick phone calls. The videos can be brief and casual. They do *not* have to be perfect—in fact, it's better if they aren't. Do this for at least thirty days straight before you decide whether this practice is worth continuing—I definitely think it is! (Remember that you can make some of these videos generic and personalize the subject line.)

Action Challenge #9: Update Your Use of Technology: If you want to evolve, become better and better, be unique and stand out, it's imperative that you incorporate new technologies and innovations into your business. This is an on-going process and should not be taken lightly. For this challenge, watch a minimum of one webinar or take one training on an aspect of technology that you know you need to improve in your business. Some excellent resources I've found are The Digital Marketer, Content Marketing Institute, and SmartInsights.com. Implement *at least one new strategy* from these trainings within the first ninety days. It might mean doing a target market ad campaign on social media or creating a landing page. Don't try to do everything at once, but master each new technology and strategy then implement the next one. Be consistent about this. If you're standing still in terms of technology, you're actually falling behind.

Action Challenge #10: Upgrade Your Marketing and Promotional Materials: Using one of your current listings, create a property brochure and a Just Listed postcard. (As before, if you don't have a current listing, you can ask a colleague if you can create materials for theirs.) Next, customize a Sellers' and/or Buyers' Guide with your contact information included. (You can find companies that provide these.) Be sure to use relevant market statistics in these guides so they are current and up to date. Don't just offer tips but include the statistics that support those tips. Include your marketing program, digital and non-digital. Create a Monthly Market Neighborhood report for an area you want to target.

Calendar dates and times to send out materials. To create location domination, I suggest a minimum of two mailings per month. When you first start, send one each week for eight consecutive weeks. Start small. Don't mail to a farm that is so large that you won't be able to afford to be consistent going forward. Add more homes to your farm as your sales increase. I went from two neighborhoods to an entire city plus half of another city within two years.

Even if they aren't your properties, you can send Just Sold and Pending in Your Neighborhood cards, as long as your colleague approves. You can also send postcards of Market Stats, Sellers' or Buyers' Tips, or "3 Things You Need to Know to Gain 12% on Your Home Sale," or "Confessions from Buyers Who Didn't Get Their Dream Home." Get creative and think about topics that would provide real value to recipients.

Think of five topics that you could put on the back of your post cards/marketing materials that would be useful for your particular neighborhood or community. It could be on fun local activities to do on weekends or where to take the kids on Spring break. How about family hot spots or three hidden restaurants for a romantic dinner? Your focus should be, "What can I do to serve them? What information will be useful to them?"

Create a brochure about you and what makes you stand out. Why should a seller or buyer hire you? Include all the innovative, tech-savvy ways you do marketing now. Include a bit about your personal story and why you chose real estate. If you have a great track record, showcase it. If you don't, showcase achievements in other areas that represent your value and work ethic.

These ten challenges will help kick-start you on your way to becoming a Community Market Leader. But you'll need to take consistent action in several areas to really see the benefits. As you set your goals and create your action plan, don't just try something a couple of times and give up on it. Innovation, implementation, and consistency are the keys to growth.

CHAPTER SEVEN

Final Note

Believe U Can

When I started putting together my training and coaching programs, I came up with an acronym to help people remember the most important parts of being a Community Market Leader. It's Believe U Can and here's how I've broken it down:

Believe: To succeed at this or just about anything in life, you need to get your head straight and keep it straight. This means noticing when your thoughts wander into negativity and cutting them off at the pass. This means infusing your brain with positive teachings from teachers like Napoleon Hill or Dale Carnegie. This means not buying into your self-doubts or letting any negative circumstance determine your attitude. You get what you think about. Think and know that you can do or be anything you want. You are the only person that can get you there or who can stop you from getting there. My new favorite book is *You Are A Badass* by Jen Sincero. The tagline is

How to Stop Doubting Your Greatness and Start Living an Awesome Life. She teaches that you can do anything no matter what it is, but you need to believe it. The book is very similar to *Think and Grow Rich*, but a little easier to understand (especially for teens). Also, *The Five Second Rule* by Mel Robbins is a book that will help you reach your goals, achieve anything you desire and overcome any obstacle you may be experiencing.

> *"There is one quality which one must possess to win, and that is definiteness of purpose, the knowledge of what one wants, and a burning desire to possess it."*
>
> —Napoleon Hill

Educate: Be an educator, not a self-promoter. First become a true expert, then share your expertise. Give people in your community information that will keep them abreast of what's happening. Give your clients information that will help them make good decisions. Be the go-to person for anyone who wants to know about your market. Show your community all the knowledge you have, share it with them. This is what sets you up to be seen as a leader.

> *"Education is for improving the lives of others and for leaving your community and the world better than you found it."*
>
> —Marian Wright Edelman

Learn: To educate others, you first have to learn enough to be a true expert—and keep learning. Tap the knowledge of mentors and coaches. Study critical areas of our business, like negotiation, technology, economic trends. Improve in areas where you're weak by taking classes, webinars, and workshops. Learning should never stop, we need to constantly learn, improve, and add to our piggy bank of knowledge.

> *"An investment in knowledge pays the best interest."*
>
> — Benjamin Franklin

Innovate: Be different! Stay in the mode of creating new ways of doing things. Use technology to reach more people, be more efficient, and get better results. Don't stick with "the ways we've always done it." Our industry hasn't changed much over the past couple of decades, but like any other industry, it has to change to survive. Find new, better, and more efficient ways of doing *everything* and never stop doing this. When everyone else is doing ABC, you do PDQ, and do it with a BANG!!

> *"If you always do what you've always done, you'll always get what you've always gotten."*
>
> —attributed to Mark Twain, Henry Ford, Tony Robbins

Engage/Everywhere: Engage your community by offering them valuable information that is relevant to them. Engage them by using video so they can feel a more personal connection. Be everywhere using social media and the internet with your informational videos, ads and listings. Let people know you before they meet you. Get personal with them. You'll see how powerful this is and how quickly you'll see the results. Engagement is equal to connection, and connection is so powerful. Think about the dynamics with your family and friends. You've built a strong connection that keeps you close. This will help you to earn trust, respect and be looked upon as a leader.

> *"Communication—the human connection—is the key to personal and career success."*
>
> —Paul J. Meyer

Value: Give real value in everything you do. Go so far above and beyond for your clients that they are thrilled to pay you. Constantly ask, "What more can I do to serve?" People are mainly concerned with themselves and what you can do for them. How can you help them? What's in it for them? Always focus on what you can *give* them. Also, stick to your own values and be impeccably ethical in all you do.

> *"Great salespeople are relationship builders who provide value and help their customers win."*
>
> —Jeffrey Gitomer

Energy/Enthusiasm: Love what you do! Tackle every project, every class, every sale as if it's your favorite thing to do. Show up with confidence that you'll do an outstanding job. Answer the phone with a smile. Show the world that you love life, you love them, and you love what you do!

> *"When you do what you love, people love what you do."*
>
> — Krista Mashore

> *"Flaming enthusiasm, backed up by horse sense and persistence, is the quality that most frequently makes for success."*
>
> —Dale Carnegie

Unique: Seek to stand out from the crowd and be different in all you do. Capitalize on your gifts and share them with the world. Being unique is what makes you memorable. If you do things like everyone else, you'll blend in and get lost in the shuffle. A CML® doesn't just blend in with the crowd. Your unique personal qualities and business practices will help you lead in your field.

> *"You are unique, and if that is not fulfilled, then something has been lost."*
>
> —Martha Graham

Courageous: Be bold and persistent. Do whatever it takes to serve your clients and reach your goals, even if it scares the heck out of you. Take each failure, learn what it can teach you, then try again. Your dreams are totally attainable. They just need a timeline and a series of smaller goals attached to them. Right now, I am pursuing my dream. I have to tell you, by doing this I am truly happier now then I've been ever. I feel so content and satisfied. I'm generally a very happy person, but it's now at a different level. I am happier in my marriage than ever before, and in my relationships with my children, friends, and peers. When you're bold enough to go after your dreams and what inspires you, it makes you show up differently in life.

> *"All our dreams can come true, if we have the courage to pursue them."*
>
> —Walt Disney

Articulate/Action: Learn to express yourself to your community and your clients. Communicate clearly and with patience, remembering that others don't have your expertise. Articulate your appreciation. And take action! Make a plan to achieve your goals and act on that plan. Be sure to implement what you learn. Work it, tweak it, adjust what you are doing and keep making it better and better. If you learn something and it doesn't work, that's okay. You will fail a few times. Get back up and eventually you'll find something that is a home run.

> *"Create a definite plan for carrying out your desire and begin at once, whether you are ready or not, to put this plan into action."*
>
> —Napoleon Hill

Niche: Don't try to be everything to everyone. Focus your business on the niche that fits you best. Learn what you need to learn to succeed in that niche. You don't have to be all things to all people. Look at what you enjoy, what you want to specialize in, and be laser focused on that. Perfect that one area and capitalize on it.

> *"Identify your niche and dominate it. And when I say dominate, I just mean work harder than anyone else could possibly work at it."*
>
> —Nate Parker

Two Final Keys: Gratitude and Persistence

I am a big believer in the power of gratitude. Research shows that gratitude is not just something for Sunday school or people who have watched *The Secret*. A recent Harvard Medical School article stated, "gratitude is strongly and consistently associated with greater happiness. Gratitude helps people feel more positive emotions, relish good experiences, improve their health, deal with adversity, and build strong relationships."

We get caught up in pursuing our goals and wanting to be better, more prosperous, and successful. There's nothing wrong with that. However, while we're doing that, it is important to be grateful for what we already have and who we already are—everything in our lives. Even if you're struggling financially, odds are that you are doing better than 93% of the world's population. And, more importantly, you have the opportunities to turn that around. Be grateful for that.

Be grateful that you ran into this book. I've offered you so many tools that will truly make a difference in your business and your life. Treat the knowledge I've shared as the gift it is and take action on it. Be grateful for whatever level of health, prosperity, and community connections you have. Marchall Sylver wrote, *"When you look for what's working in your life, it expands."*

Take nothing for granted—your family, your friends, your opportunities, your well-being. Appreciate the life you've been given and all that you've experienced. If you feel inclined to whine and complain about something, knock it off! Wallowing in regrets or "if only's" never got anyone anywhere. Step into the attitude of gratitude and notice what a difference it makes.

And be persistent.

You might have read some of my suggestions and thought, "Oh, that's way out of my comfort zone. I could never do that." Well, yes, you can. Keep your "why" in front of you as you continue to learn and take action on what you're learning. If you keep on doing what you've always done, you'll keep on getting what you've always gotten.

Often, as you're about to master something new or you're very close to the end result you want, that's exactly when it gets the toughest. Many people back off when their business is just about to turn the corner. Don't stop. Keep on going.

When Winston Churchill had to lead Great Britain through World War II, he often had to encourage his country to never give up despite terrible setbacks. He said, *"Success consists of going from failure to failure without loss of enthusiasm."* Dale Carnegie wrote, *"A quitter never wins and a winner never quits."* And there's a Japanese proverb that says, *"Nanakorobi yaoki,"* which means, *"Fall down seven times and stand up eight."* Anyone who has achieved success will tell you that you just need to keep putting one foot in front of the other, no matter what.

Thank you for spending your precious time reading this book. I hope you will use what I've shared to achieve all you desire.

Sincerely,

Krista Mashore

Krista Mashore

Be sure to visit **www.sell100homesbook.com** for free resources that will help you grow and automate your real estate business.

Resources

You have access to many resources to support you on your journey to becoming a highly successful Community Market Leader! In this section, I will share some of my favorites, the resources that propelled me to the success I enjoy today.

Books I Recommend

Here's a list of books that have been particularly important to me. Some are classics and some are more recent. Personally, I use audio books so I have a constant stream of good information and inspiration.

Think and Grow Rich by Napoleon Hill

The 10X Rule by Grant Cardone

How to Win Friends and Influence People by Dale Carnegie

You Are A Badass by Jen Sincero

Mindset: The New Psychology of Success by Carol Dweck

The Power of Consistency by Weldon Long

How To Master The Art of Selling by Tom Hopkins

The Thank You Economy by Gary Vaynerchuk

The Go Giver by Bob Berg and John David Mann

The 5 Second Rule: Transform your Life, Work, and Confidence with Everyday Courage by Mel Robbins

Credentials

Having lots of letters after your name is impressive. But what's more important is all you learn in the process. Here are some of the credentials I've earned and why I think they're important.

- **MCNE: Master Certified Negotiations Expert:** (fewer than .05% of Realtors® nationwide have this certification) Teaches the art of negotiations for a win-win for everyone while protecting your clients' best interests and outcomes.

- **CNE: Certified Negotiations Expert:** (fewer than 3% of Realtors® nationwide have this certification) Required prior to MCNE.

- **GRI: Graduate Realtor® Institute** (fewer than 3% of Realtors® nationwide have this certification) This is like getting a Master's or Doctorate degree in Real Estate. You need to have sold a certain number of homes, to have been in the business for a certain number of years, or to have completed certain college requirements prior to applying and getting into the program. This credential sets you apart as having a high standard of professionalism and knowledge in the business.

- **CRS: Council of Residential Specialist** (fewer than 3% of Realtors® nationwide hold this credential) You earn this credential by taking advanced classroom courses, self-paced e-learning, live webinars, and attending other events that help you stay on top of the competitive and changing real estate environment. You must also demonstrate outstanding performance in residential real estate. This is the elite of the elite in residential real estate.

- **CHSA: Certified Home Selling Adviser**

- **CHBA: Certified Home Buying Adviser**

ILHM: Institute for Luxury Home Marketing: The Institute for Luxury Home Marketing is focused on the specific skills and tools necessary to be successful in the upper-tier residential market.

BPOR: Broker's Price Opinion Resource: This program trains you to properly price and evaluate properties as an appraiser would.

LDPD: Luxury Depressed Property Expert Distinguished Designation: This training teaches you how to showcase all properties, including properties with less desirable qualities, to gain maximum exposure and pricing for the seller.

e-Pro: Technology Designation: Training for this designation teaches you to digitally market your listings for maximum exposure to buyers who may or may not be looking at properties.

I earned several of my degrees years ago to become an expert in dealing with homes affected by the real estate market crash. These credentials aren't relevant to me today, however, they allowed me to be highly effective during that period:

ASD: Accredited Short Sale Certified

CDPE: Certified Distressed Property Expert

SFR: Short Sale Foreclosure Resource

PSC: Pre-Foreclosure Specialist

CHS: Certified Hafa Specialist

5-Star Short Sale Certified

Resinet Certified

Equator Certified

NAR Resources

The National Association of REALTORS® website has a ton of useful information. If you've never looked at it, just go to NAR. org. You'll find all kinds of news, blogs, and videos. For example, currently they have a blog on *Drones, The Appraiser's Next Great Tool.* The site also has R.S.S. feeds with more information and tools, charts and graphs, research and statistics. You can use any of this information to shine as a Community Market Leader in your own videos and presentations. Just be sure to give the NAR credit when you do. NAR.org also has apps you can download. For example, a calculator that shows people how much they can save per year in taxes from their mortgage interest write-off. I encourage you to look through the site and see what it has to offer—then come up with innovative ways to use it in your business.

Specific Resources to Stay Current

Here are some resources to help you keep on top of the news and trends that matter. Some of these are real estate related, others are for general business and the economy. A few will help you keep current with marketing and consumer trends. I suggest you check them out, then bookmark the ones that appeal to you so you can tap into them on a consistent basis.

- Inman News
- CNBC.com/real-estate
- Keeping Current Matters- Real Estate
- Paperless Agent
- Facebook groups like Lab Coat Agents and Club Wealth Real Estate Agents Institute
- National Association of REALTORS®, NAR.org

- Your state real estate association
- Content Marketing Institute

Through these resources, you'll also learn about conferences, online classes, and webinars that can be useful.

Helpful Forms and Examples

First, here are some links to show you some of the materials I use. Pay attention to the level of quality we use. You can use whatever you'd like, but be sure to make it your own and *improve* on it! I've included things like my Buyers' Tour Package, Seller's Checklist, an avatar worksheet and some example emails.

To download these materials, Be sure to visit
www.sell100homesbook.com for free resources
that will help you grow and automate your real
estate business.

You are welcome to customize these for your own use—just make sure you understand them and know how to apply them correctly.

For more information on working directly with Krista
Go to **www.KristaMashore.com**

About the Author

Realtor®, author, trainer and coach **Krista Mashore** developed a highly successful real estate career in Northern California before turning her attention to sharing the secrets to her success through her writing, coaching and trainings.

Krista began her career in education, teaching elementary school and earning her Master's degree in Curriculum and Instruction on her way to becoming a principal. But in 2001, she chose to switch gears and pursue a career in real estate. Krista sold 69 homes in her very first year in the business and has averaged well over 100 homes every year since, earning her a spot in the Top 1% of Realtors® in the nation.

Krista's innovative approach flies in the face of conventional wisdom about how Realtors® should promote themselves and market their listings. She credits her success to her consistent drive for growth and learning, and applying the best practices and cutting edge technologies major corporations use. Through her books, coaching, webinars and courses, Krista now offers step-by-step instruction so others can achieve that same success.

Krista lives in Northern California with her husband and three teenaged children. An active member of her community, her latest project is *Teens Lifting Lives*, a mentoring and peer support group that gives young people the tools and encouragement they need to achieve their own success.

"The reason I love continually learning is that I know there's a better, more effective way to do almost anything—even if you're already good at that thing. That's why I dive into situations that might stretch my thinking and challenge how I do things. Learning even one small thing each day allows me to keep expanding into the next 'better way.' As importantly, I implement that better way and continue to improve on it."

—Krista Mashore

Made in the USA
Coppell, TX
31 July 2023

19805172R00118